Removing the Stalin Stain

Marxism and the Working Class in the Twenty-First Century

Removing the Stalin Stain

Marxism and the Working Class in the Twenty-First Century

William Briggs

Winchester, UK
Washington, USA

JOHN HUNT PUBLISHING

First published by Zero Books, 2020
Zero Books is an imprint of John Hunt Publishing Ltd., No. 3 East St., Alresford,
Hampshire SO24 9EE, UK
office@jhpbooks.com
www.johnhuntpublishing.com
www.zero-books.net

For distributor details and how to order please visit the 'Ordering' section on our website.

ISBN: 978 1 78904 521 5
978 1 78904 522 2 (ebook)
Library of Congress Control Number: 2019951220

A CIP catalogue record for this book is available from the British Library.

Design: Stuart Davies

UK: Printed and bound by CPI Group (UK) Ltd, Croydon, CR0 4YY
US: Printed and bound by Thomson-Shore, 7300 West Joy Road, Dexter, MI 48130

We operate a distinctive and ethical publishing philosophy in
all areas of our business, from our global network of authors to
production and worldwide distribution.

Contents

Also by William Briggs

Classical Marxism in an Age of Capitalist Crisis: The Past is
Prologue

For Rose

Introduction

This is a book about ideas and about taking sides in the battle of ideas. It is partisan and at times polemic. This is not a disclaimer. It is a simple statement of intent. In the final analysis that intent is to promote and defend Marxism and especially classical Marxism. There is more than a hint in that remark of a degree of 'debate' about the term Marxism.

There are innumerable schools of 'Marxist' thought. In fact, there is quite a 'shopping list', including Western, Structural, Neo, Frankfurt School, Autonomist, Humanist, Feminist and post-Marxist Marxism, which is surely more than enough to be going on with. There will be moments in the following pages when individual schools will be referred to, but I hope that a generic 'Marxism', in inverted commas, will suffice, or sometimes a catch-all 'contemporary' Marxist label. Wherever the term Marxist appears without inverted commas, I am referring to classical Marxist theory and practice.

Agreement and ideas do not always fit together smoothly. Ideas and dissent are a closer fit. If we were to break the world of ideas and ideology down to its most elemental parts, we might, at a push, just agree that there are ultimately two big ideas – that represented by capitalist ideology and that which might variously be called socialist ideology or Marxism. I won't push my luck any further. That is surely enough agreement for the moment. I place my arguments firmly within the school of Marxism that happily wears the label classical Marxism.

To observe the world, even casually, is to observe a world marked by conflict, crisis and contradiction. There are things that ought to be blindingly obvious and yet it is the refusal to acknowledge objective realities, or worse, a desire to distort such realities, that has allowed capitalism and its state to remain free from serious challenge. Capitalism is a globalising force. This is just one objective truth. The nation-state remains central to the management of capitalism. This is another. The contradiction between these two truths is the ultimate contradiction that faces capitalism and the people in the twenty-first century. If capitalism must grow and expand, then it is obvious that globalisation and an integration of capitalism must follow. Night, after all, tends to follow day. If the capitalist state has the role of administering capitalist relations within defined national borders, then it is equally obvious that conflict and contradiction will grow. Why the problem has not been resolved and why it cannot be resolved is a central focus of this book.

The two 'big' ideas stand in stark opposition to one another. On the one hand is capitalism, both as an economic formation and as a philosophical construct. On the other, stands Marxism, again both as an economic and philosophical construct. The two ideas have occupied something of a shared space and have remained as opposing forces since capital became the dominant paradigm and since Marx and Engels gave voice to an oppositional, revolutionary perspective. The fact that capitalism has maintained its dominance, despite being beset by unresolvable contradictions, has led many to suppose that it is either inherently superior to its ideological foe, or that Marxism is in some way a flawed theory.

I argue that there is a dual crisis that affects both capitalism and Marxism. Marxism's crisis evolved alongside capitalism's and developed throughout the twentieth century as capitalism managed to resist the destructive and existential crises that assailed it. How this came about and what can be done to resolve these crises is the pivot around which this work revolves. While the crises and contradictions of capitalism have been famously outlined by Marx and elaborated on by subsequent 'Marxist' theoreticians and activists, this book draws particular attention to a final and fundamental contradiction of capitalism. This contradiction is the ultimate and irrevocable contradiction.

It is the contradiction between a globalising and increasingly integrated capitalism and the nation-state system. The nation-state remains central to governance and to maintaining order and structure within the world but is effectively an obstacle to an inevitable globalisation of capital.

It's nothing personal

While this is a book about ideas, its ultimate purpose is to promote one specific idea. A book about ideas inevitably bumps into and confronts the individuals who have articulated those ideas. It is a very short and slippery journey of a very few steps from discussing an idea, to discussing the individual associated with that idea, to sliding into subjectivity. As much as is possible, I have avoided the subjective. While Stalinism occupies a significant space, Stalin does not. The same applies to other central characters whose thoughts have framed the arguments that follow. Marx, Engels, Lenin, Trotsky have all been subjected to endless biographies and have suffered (or benefited) accordingly. Having said that, it is difficult to stand apart and untouched by the distortions, stain and shadow that Stalinism cast and still casts today. Stalin has been dead now for over 65 years and it would be best if his ideas mouldered along with his bones. Regimes that once proclaimed their Stalinist credentials are no more, or rather, have mutated into something quite else. His adherents (those who still cling to the cult of Stalin) skulk in ever shrinking and ineffectual bands. However, Stalinism and its legacy continues to haunt the Marxist movement. The spectre of Stalin and Stalinism has been so successfully invoked as to make many shy away from Marxism, even though the two ideas stand as polar opposites.

Personalities, no matter how we might try, are never far from the surface. The media and, unfortunately too many, theorists and historians promote the personal, whereby personality becomes almost an alternative to analysis. There can be no room for the personal in such a work as this. What developed in those years following the Russian Revolution, and how 'Marxism' became Stalinised, was not at the whim of an individual. Rather, it was organically related to a political tendency that existed and pre-dated that very revolution. It was an international tendency within Marxism and had already surfaced in the split in Marxism that preceded World War I. It represented a form of labour reformism that was tied to a nationalist outlook that grew in strength as the Russian Revolution struggled to gain global traction.

Even if Stalin had not appeared, many of the same political distortions would have emerged in the post-Lenin period. This proposition may appear to be at odds with conventional wisdom but to suppose that the degeneration of Marxism in the Soviet Union was in any way the work of an individual defies logic. Whether the political tendency represented by Stalin could have been countered remains an intense point of debate but is not the subject of this discussion. The fact is that a Marxist party was quickly usurped by a bureaucratic 'party'. Stalinism was a political response and reaction against Marxism. It was a nationalist response to internationalism. This, it must be remembered, is at the heart of the 'great contradiction' that motivates this book.

Those who seek a better world, free from exploitation, from inequality and from capitalism, have long lived in the shadow of Stalinism. Marxism, as the antithesis of capitalism, has been weakened, its theory distorted by Stalinism and then further disabled by many who have tried to 'rescue' Marxism. Each 'rescue mission' has weakened the theory and removed it from any real sense of practice. The practitioners of Marxism – the 'activist' Marxists – have, in turn, suffered from a theory that has, in reality, disarmed them. The result has seen the world slide further and further into a morass. Stalinism, and its intensely anti-Marxist theories and practices, played and still plays a significant role and one which assists capitalism to remain unchallenged.

The twentieth century began with a crisis in capitalism. The contradictions so evident in capitalism were in no way resolved in the century that followed. The decades came and went, and capitalism remained as mired in crisis as ever it was. There is a difference, however, and that difference is that the crisis is deeper and more intractable. The world is threatened by war, inequality has grown, the middle class has begun to shrink, the working class, especially in the developed economies, has been atomised, and the crisis of capitalism is steadily devouring the planet. But despite all of this, capitalism maintains its place of dominance. It lurches and lumbers on its destructive path. Nobody can reasonably claim that capitalism is delivering.

The beginning of the twentieth century was also marked by a growing crisis in Marxism. As the century rolled on, that crisis developed – almost as a macabre echo of the growing crisis in capitalism, or as a crisis that evolved alongside the crisis of capitalism. While conjecture and uncertainty affect so many things, there are also certainties. The first of these is that 'Marxism's' crisis has aided and abetted capitalism's capacity to survive. The second is that Stalinism throughout the twentieth century all but destroyed Marxism. Capital, it must be said, owes a huge debt to Stalin and his heirs.

The twentieth century was a grim time for Marxism, in both its theoretical and practical manifestations. Far too many theoreticians who laboured, and still do, under the banner of 'Marxism' have tried, feebly or valiantly (depending on the degree of charity that might be in the heart of the observer) to make Marx 'relevant' in the face of this or that shift and turn of capitalism. Each 'rescue mission' has seen the core values that underpin Marxist theory diminish and, over time, that which can be described as 'contemporary' Marxism has become a mere shadow or caricature of the 'spectre' that once stalked Europe and the world. While the theoretical structure became increasingly debased, the activist forms of Marxism, the practitioners, appeared ever more removed from the class they purported to support. And yet, despite all this, the crisis of capitalism compels more and more people to regard socialism and Marxism in a positive light. Recent polls in the US showed that 61 per cent of young Americans now recognise that socialism is preferable to capitalism. A good idea just won't go away.

Problems and crises

It has become almost axiomatic to speak of the 'crisis of capitalism'. Marx in *Capital Vol. 1* (1986a: 266) identified three primary elements of capitalism: the concentration of the means of production into relatively few hands, the social nature of labour and the development of a world market. These elements necessarily act in contradiction to one another and in the twenty-first century, globalisation, as an expression of the 'world market', is especially relevant. Crisis, for Marx, was an inescapable component of capitalism.

Marxism, with its materialist view of economics and history, is uniquely positioned to analyse this concept of contradiction. Contradiction can, of course, simply indicate a set of contrasting ideas or statements. Marx, in *The Poverty of Philosophy*, argued that 'what constitutes dialectical movement is the co-existence of two contradictory sides, their conflict and their fusion into a new category' (1956: 126). Marx's primary use of the term was connected to his analysis of the historical process of capitalism, the private ownership of productive forces and the social character of production. In this sense contradiction is necessarily antagonistic.

The underlying contradictions within capitalism have not been and cannot be resolved so long as capitalism exists. Consequently, it is necessary to draw attention to the interaction of these contradictions. The intensification of capitalist globalisation can be linked to irresolvable contradictions stemming, in part, from a tendency for profit rates to fall, which, in turn, drives capitalist expansion.

The arguments that underpin this work are framed by Marxist analysis. The strength of this approach lies in Marxism's integrated historical and materialist approach. The fact that capitalist globalisation has been occurring at such a rapid pace is both logical and explicable if viewed from such a materialistic outlook. Marx and Engels, in the *Communist Manifesto*, recognised that 'the bourgeoisie cannot exist without constantly revolutionising the instruments of production, and therefore the relations of production, and with them the whole relations of society' (1977: 38-39).

Gyorgi Lukacs, decades later, declared that:

historical materialism eclipses all the methods that went before it, on the one hand, inasmuch as it conceives reality as a historical process, and on the other hand, inasmuch as it is in a position to understand the starting point of knowledge at any one time. Knowledge itself is understood to be just as much a product of the objective process of history (2000: 105).

The truth that lies behind that assumption has been given greater credence as the crisis in capitalism has developed. This work, then, adopts a process that might be described as theory building, or what might be more appropriately labelled as the promotion of an already perfectly valid theory that has been allowed to fall into disrepair. This approach offers an understanding of capitalist development, globalisation and crisis, as well as the problems and ideological weaknesses that have afflicted Marxism. Analysing how and why Marxism became so mired in discontent does not discredit, but enriches Marxist theory. It allows us to discard that which is unnecessary in favour of integrating, if and where possible, new insights into a working theory.

Capitalism has, from the beginning, been enmeshed in irresolvable contradictions. These contradictions have at once promoted capitalism's forward motion while acting, over time, to deepen the contradictions inherent in the system. Among these contradictions are: the private ownership of the means of production and the social nature of the production process; the drive to maximise profit by expanding the productive processes and surplus value, which necessitates limiting real wages growth; the imperative to increase labour productivity contributing to the tendency for profit rates to fall; and the drive to a globalised economy while relying on the nation-state system to administer capitalist relations. At the same time, and as a response to the expansionary nature of capitalism, its progressive role, as described by Marx in the nineteenth century, has long since disappeared. What remains unchanged is its motivation of survival. It has maintained and used the state admirably in this quest for long life.

Marxism maintains that a primary purpose of the state is to facilitate capitalist development. While the role of the state has not fundamentally altered, capitalism's development has necessarily placed a strain on that relationship. This first became apparent as capitalism quickly outgrew the nation-state and, more recently, has transformed itself into a globalised entity. Marx's view of the nation-state and of its future was clear. He maintained that the development and expansion of capitalism would ultimately weaken any semblance of independence for the state (Dunn 2009: 158, Renton 2005: 16-17).

The entwined issues of globalisation, nationalism, the state and capitalism remain. Crisis and contradiction abound and frame the daily lives of the people on this planet, regardless of whether such contradictions are recognised. Unravelling and cutting this Gordian knot is the task of Marxist theory and practice. Marxism was formed, after all, not simply to explain the world but to change it. That challenge remains, and it will be argued that a classical Marxist approach is ultimately the way to achieve that end.

Aims and motivations

While this book seeks to 'do' a number of things, it ultimately has one overarching aim. That aim is to present the case for Marxism and to place a classical perspective at the heart of on-going debates and polemics within 'Marxism'. The work attempts this by addressing the problem and issue of how to resolve the great contradiction between an increasing and inevitable integration of global capitalism and capitalism's requirement of a strong system of nation-states that act as an administrator and facilitator of capitalist development.

In seeking to achieve that aim, I shall focus on the short-comings and the 'crisis' that has so afflicted Marxist theory and practice during the past century. Capitalism, riven by crisis and contradiction, remains largely without challenge. The interconnected nature of these two issues lies at the heart of the book. For many decades, contemporary Marxist theorists have sought to make Marxism 'relevant' in the face of capitalism's apparent 'resilience'. Each step that the theorists have taken has been a step away from the core elements and values of Marxism.

'Marxist' scholars and analysts from the late 1920s and 1930s sought to 'save' the theory. Joseph Femia (2007) describes this variously as a rescue mission against Stalinism, or from an intellectual movement away from western Europe, or as a response to lost opportunities after the Russian Revolution. Perry Anderson (1979) argues that ultimately these 'rescuers' reflected a sense of defeatism.

In any event, these moves distanced successive theorists, not just from the sterile terrain of Stalinism, but significantly from the essential elements that denote Marxist theory: the pivotal importance of the working class, the fact that political action is a product of economic stimulus, and that nationalist responses to global questions will always be ineffectual.

Another motivation in writing this book is to address the problems of the contradiction between an integrated and globalised capitalism and the on-going necessity for a system of nation-states. This final and fundamental contradiction of capitalism is the most urgent problem and yet it remains poorly represented in an expanding literature that seeks to describe problems in capitalism and in Marxism. As the crisis in capitalism develops and sharpens, there has been a resurgence in nationalist responses – politically and economically. The future of any emancipatory programme must be framed by a response to this problem.

There is a direct, almost causal link in the evolution of the crisis in 'Marxism' and in its seeming incapacity to respond to the crisis that is so evident in the capitalist system. That 'causal moment' is the moment of the Stalinisation of Marxism. Capitalism was the ultimate winner from the distortion that Stalinism engendered. Subsequent manoeuvres by an ever-expanding and divergent set of contemporary Marxist theorists have further weakened the capacity to advance a theory that could provide a leadership for the working class, confront capitalism and effect fundamental economic and political change.

The relevance of Marxism for the twenty-first century

Marxism's historical development has been marked by dislocation. It is a sad truth, but a truth just the same. It is important to isolate and analyse the fractures that have so weakened the theory and the practice of Marxism. While the role that Stalinism played (and still plays) has been central to the developing crisis in Marxism, it must be remembered that many ostensibly non-Stalinist or anti-Stalinist theorists have, in reaction to the depredations of Stalinism, progressively shifted the focus of the theory away from the central role of the working class, from a consistently internationalist approach, and from ascribing primary importance to the fact that economic issues inform political responses.

At the same time, capitalism has not been able to overcome its inherent contradictions or its potential for crisis. From the 1970s on, this tendency to crisis has become even more acute. Globalisation of capitalist relations and production has become ever more pronounced as a qualitative change in capitalism becomes evident. Simultaneously, the nation-state remains integral to capitalist development. This contradiction, this dilemma, has given rise to a growth in nationalist sentiments, in economic nationalism, in right and left populism and in an inevitable rise in insecurity. In discussing, describing and analysing this irresolvable contradiction, I operate within a clearly defined framework of dialectical and historical materialism.

This book, then, consciously seeks to develop a theoretical response to this contradiction. In doing so it re-asserts the relevance of Marxism, not only in its explanatory form, but as a means of promoting organisational structures that will challenge the rule of capitalism and offer a realisable path to fundamental political and economic change. It is in such a context that the book assumes a direct and immediate relevance. It is all but impossible to argue against the proposition that capitalism is in crisis and that the crisis is unable to be resolved, without fundamental change being effected.

The logic of capitalist development is clear. Marx and, it must be acknowledged, economists before him wrote of the tendency for profit rates to fall. Capitalism, in seeking to forestall this, and to survive, has been compelled to break free from any fetters that national boundaries might impose. This drive towards globalisation has been an integral part of capitalist development ever since capitalism emerged. There has been an almost symbiotic relationship between the state and capital.

Each needed the other and the state rapidly became a facilitator for capitalist development. None of this is earth-shattering. It is clear, evidential and follows a logical path.

Marxism grew and developed alongside capitalism. The logic of capitalist development was obvious to the early Marxist thinkers. They were clear that global responses were required to resolve global issues. After all, perhaps the first Marxist slogan was that 'the working men have no country'. The decades since that slogan was first advanced have seen Marxist theory buffeted by events and by theorists who have become, at best, reactive to events. The world economy was globalising at an accelerated rate in the period before World War I. The contradiction that largely motivates this book was never sharper than at that moment in history. On the one hand was the inexorable global march of an integrating capitalism. On the other was the reaction from national capital, nation-states and the rhetoric that fuelled the drive to war. The majority of those who might have been called Marxist abandoned the essential internationalism of the theory and coalesced around national flags and symbols. It is hardly a stretch of the imagination to suggest that there are obvious similarities in today's globalisation of capital and the corresponding rise of economic nationalism, left and right populism and the renewed symbolism of the 'nation'. Marxism assumes a special significance and relevance when viewed against such a backdrop and so too do the ideas that this book promotes.

The book also has a direct relevance in that it seeks to contribute to debates within contemporary Marxism. It is necessary to appreciate the trajectory of the anti-capitalist, 'Marxist' movement since the period of the Russian Revolution, the Stalinisation of Marxism and the attempts to make Marxism 'relevant' by subsequent contemporary Marxist theorists, which have led, inexorably, to a further weakening of that theory. It is also necessary to appreciate the depth of that 'Stalin stain' and the unconscious influence that it has exerted and still does on the working class, its economic and political organisations and on perceptions of the state, nation and internationalism. What must follow is a re-arming of the working class with political organisation that is independent, internationalist and motivated by Marxist theory. Addressing these issues makes this work relevant for the present and into the immediate future.

Chapter 1

In the midst of crisis

Capitalism is subject to irreconcilable crisis and contradiction which has both driven it forward and threatened its very existence. As Trotsky (1953: 61-62) observed, capitalism lives by crises and booms. He likened the cycle to the inward and outward breath of a human being. He was talking specifically about conditions as they were in the 1920s. His observations are not only still relevant but are more acutely relevant. The only difference is that the 'breathing' more resembles that of a patient with emphysema. It has become more laboured and shallow as crisis follows crisis in ever shorter periods and the observable crisis becomes that little deeper. The observation of crisis is not, however, a one-way street. Marxism, too, is riven by crisis and contention. This is a sad but inescapable fact. Despite the depth of this contention, Marxism remains not merely relevant, but central to combatting and replacing capitalism. Marxism's 'road to crisis' parallels the development of capitalist crisis but has that extra layer to contend with – the ideologically crippling movement that has increasingly seen 'Marxist' theory reacting to events rather than acting in any proactive manner.

If Marxism remains relevant and if it remains central to combatting capitalism, then it needs not only defence but validation. This can be done in four connected steps. The first is to promote a classical Marxist approach that presents an essentially optimistic view of the world. The second is to briefly examine the essence of Marxism as both theory and practice. This flows into the third step which engages with long-held but divisive arguments as to whether Marxism provides a 'scientific' view of the world and its development. A final step is taken by a short exploration of the weaknesses that have emerged in contemporary Marxist theory and of the Stalinist genesis of these weaknesses.

It is important to draw on a classical interpretation of Marxist theory that provides an optimistic view of the world and of its economic and political future. Such an exploration points to Marxism's critique of capitalism as an expanding, globalising system. It focuses on the historically combative nature of Marxism and of its goal to challenge and displace capitalism. History allows for an appreciation of how ideological dislocation developed in Marxist thought throughout the twentieth century and how such discontent drew far too many to question the relevance of Marxism as a means of opposing capitalism. We are still living in the shadow of this ideological dislocation. The ghost of Stalin still haunts Marxism.

It is also necessary to reflect on the development of Marxist crises that grew out of early attempts to 'improve' or 'revise' Marxist theory. Much of the latter disputation and conflict within Marxism echoes earlier polemics, and, in particular, the question of whether a reformist or revolutionary path ought to be followed.

Such analysis, based in and around a classical Marxist perspective, establishes an historical and theoretical platform upon which the substantial arguments that motivate this book rest.

There is plenty of room for optimism

Marxists come in for all manner of criticism and some of it appears to be more than justifiable. This is made more obvious when almost every possible permutation of what has happened, is happening, might happen, has had a 'Marxist' interpretation placed upon it, or if truth be told, any number of 'Marxist' interpretations. It would seem that anybody offering a view that is in any way contrary to that of the dominant paradigm can either be labelled a 'Marxist', or conversely can self-apply the label 'Marxist' to just about any form of analysis. Emmanuel Wallerstein's (1986) comment about the emergence of a thousand Marxisms in the post-World War II period is sadly apt. There are many Marxist schools of thought, Marxist analyses of just about everything in every area of physical or mental endeavour, and doubtless in areas yet to be imagined. Marxist critiques flourish, not only of capitalism, but of every permutation of every social issue, real or imagined, let alone critiques of other Marxist theories. None of us, it would seem, are safe! There are a dizzying array of texts, conferences, papers and commentaries from legions of ever more shrill and discordant 'Marxist' thinkers and writers.

So, it is no wonder that Marxists come in for criticism, but to be criticised for being optimistic might stretch the bounds of good manners. If we look at the world as it is, then there would seem to be little to be optimistic about. We see economies in crisis, a concentration of wealth into fewer hands, stagnating and shrinking wages, and social and political fragmentation that is affecting developed and developing states alike. Inequality has risen sharply. Social cohesion has weakened. Any serious attempts to counter-pose other ideas and especially concepts of socialism are muted at best. What then is there to feel optimistic about?

Part of the answer, the secret if you will, lies in Marx's materialist conception of history. It is, after all, the foundation upon which Marxism is built and offers an intensely optimistic worldview. It argues that the movement of history is predicated upon a dialectical clash of opposing forces. These forces are represented by the existence of classes and in the class nature of society. The interests of these opposing forces cannot be reconciled without fundamental changes to the political and economic structures of society. Marx argued that these antagonisms must inevitably translate into class struggle that, in turn, would result in a new economic and social order.

It is not enough, however, to make broad statements, as edicts or proclamations. All propositions must be able to be defended. Everything that can be defined as 'Marxist' has been polemicised, almost to the point of death. Some of the sharpest critiques against Marxist theory have taken aim at what has been described as its 'determinism'. The critics, who incidentally include more than a few 'Marxists', argue that the most basic premises upon which the theory rests – the base/superstructure nature of society, that economics informs political responses, that class matters, that historical materialism does explain the trajectory of society – are somehow 'fundamentalist' in nature and get in the way of making Marxism relevant for the modern age. These arguments cannot be simply waved away. They are central to this discussion. For the moment, however, we need to allow Marxist theory to be explained by Marxist theorists, with Marx being the most obvious starting point.

In his *Contribution to the Critique of Political Economy*, Marx (1918: 11-12) argued that social existence determines consciousness and that through social production people enter into sets of relationships that are independent of their own will. What Marx did was to describe how society operated and how the class relationships of that society were central to how society operated. He showed that the aspirations of classes are necessarily antagonistic to one another. He also showed that these relations were transitory. He maintained that economic formations and society advanced in accordance with the materialist conception of history. The capitalist mode of production with its inherent contradictions and antagonisms is an integral part of this process, because, 'the productive forces developing in the womb of bourgeois society create the material conditions for the solution of that antagonism' (Marx 1918: 13).

There is a simple and appealing logic that underpins Marxist theory. It was, after all, a theory that was meant to be read and understood by the broadest layers of society and particularly the working class. Not surprisingly then, Marx summarised his contribution to the development of political ideas in three succinct points. These were that social classes were simply stages in historical development, that the class struggle necessarily leads to the 'dictatorship of the proletariat' and that this, too, is a transitional stage towards the creation of a communist society that would promote the free development of the individual. Sitting alongside this, we have Marxist philosophy and economic theory that emphasises the interaction between social classes, changes in material conditions, how society is organised and of the primacy of economic factors over political ones as engines for change.

Marxism is ultimately an optimistic worldview, but Marx was not some nineteenth century Pollyanna. Marxism promises something and promotes action to achieve positive and far-reaching outcomes. Capitalism might well be a destructive force, but it is not an immutable force. Marx viewed the world from a highly partisan perspective. It was a position framed by an understanding of the class nature of society and of the inequality that such divisions breed (Marx and Engels 1977: 48). Capitalism, for Marx, was an engine of growth that both revolutionised productive forces while simultaneously driving millions into poverty. Marx's vision was that the machinery of capitalism would be taken and used for the needs of humanity and not for private wealth.

Marx and Engels understood capitalism to be a globalising force. This has intense significance when considered against the backdrop of capitalist development in the twenty-first century. Renton (2005: 9-10) draws a connection between Marx and Engels' work and modern globalisation theorists, recognising that states and regions were being affected by developments in the global economy. The two wrote of the disorder and crisis that capitalism engenders and of the contradictions that lead to economic crisis. Capitalism and the bourgeoisie, in seeking to manage these critical moments, react and respond by engaging in:

> on the one hand enforced destruction of a mass of productive forces; on the other, by the conquest of new markets, and by the more thorough exploitation of the old ones. That is to say, by paving the way for more extensive and more destructive crises, and by diminishing the means whereby crises are prevented (Marx and Engels 1977: 42).

Central to the approach of classical Marxism was the belief that socialism must be constructed as a world system and not be confined within national borders. Such a foundational premise was based on the knowledge that capitalism was already moving beyond the limitations of nation-states. Capitalism was impelled towards globalisation precisely because of its very 'nature' and because of its internal contradictions. Marx and Engels famously stated that 'the need of a constantly expanding market for its products chases the bourgeoisie over the whole surface of the globe. It must nestle everywhere, settle everywhere, establish connexions everywhere' (1977: 39).

Something happened on the way to the end of capitalism. Marxist theory, it must be remembered, was predicated on the eruption of class struggle, the breakdown of capitalist economics and the replacement of capitalism with socialism. An international movement was built upon these foundations and there was every expectation that Marx and Engels' theories would, in a relatively short time, come to fruition. It was a theory intimately connected with practice and in this context was fraught with potential difficulties. It was, after all, an ideological perspective that existed in the real world and in real time. Something happened. Capitalism did not collapse. A global socialist system did not eventuate. Where socialist revolutions occurred, there were mutations and counter-revolutions. For some this 'proved' the superiority of capitalism. For others, it showed a fundamental flaw in Marxist theory.

Capitalism's continued existence seemed to question the validity of central elements of Marxism. The developing and on-going polemics and disputes among Marxists were hardly surprising. This is especially obvious as those same adherents of Marxism lived and worked in an atmosphere infused with bourgeois ideology that was exacerbated by disappointment and missed opportunities. While this is an undeniable reality, the sense of optimism remains. Why? To understand this, it is first necessary to understand the essence of Marxism and of Marxist analysis.

The world through Marxist eyes

There are moments when we are forced to use all-encompassing terms like 'Marxism'. It can become irritating because there are so many 'Marxisms' jostling for space in the market-place of ideas and each, while sharing something, are at odds with most others. It would be so much easier with the stroke of a pen or keyboard to rid the discussion of irritating variants that cloud the issue, but we must, it seems, live with the inconvenience. Or must we? If Marxism exists in order to change the world, then ideas that serve to weaken, diminish or distort the message of Marxism must be combatted. Ideas, after all, matter.

At the same time 'Marxists' of most shades can broadly accept that Marxism, for all its difficulties, and however poorly used, remains the best vehicle by which to understand and analyse issues of the state, globalisation, relations between state and capital and, in a limited manner, the place and role of the working class. Regardless of this truth, nobody should expect this uneasy 'alliance' to hold for more than a second. The disparate forces quickly diverge. After all, it is a battle of ideas.

Understanding how things operate is one thing. Setting about changing things is quite another. A unified theory encapsulating economic, political and social factors is essential for first understanding but then, importantly, resolving the contradiction between the growth of global capitalism as an economic focus, and the nation-state as a vehicle for political organisation. A Marxist perspective provides such an approach and stands in stark contradistinction to an expanding range of 'anti-capitalist' theories, and especially against the distortions that Stalinism has imposed on Marxist theory and practice.

If we had to choose a single word that cuts to the core of Marxist analysis, then that word might well be 'connectivity'. Daniel Little, for instance, illustrates this point by isolating a number of separate themes in *Capital Volume 1*. These include descriptions of the property relations and production within capitalism, a development of the theory of labour value, a model of the capitalist mode of production, of how the competitive market operates, an analysis of both the social and economic implications of these features, a sociological account of the reproduction of property relations, an historical account of how these relations were established in a pre-capitalist society, as well as a description of contemporary life and conditions for the working class (Little 1986: 18).

Marx's method is one that synthesises the components of capitalist relations, beginning with the role of labour and concluding with the development of globalisation. Marx, in his *Grundrisse*, explained that what was essential was to make observations that move from the simple to the complex and that show the inter-relationship of all component parts:

> simple conceptions such as labour, division of labour, demand, exchange value, and conclude with state, international exchange and world market...The concrete is concrete because it is a combination of many determinations, i.e. a unity of diverse elements. In our thought it therefore appears as a process of synthesis, as a result, and not as a starting

point, although it is the real starting point and, therefore, also the starting point of observation and conception (1974: 100-101).

'The relations of production of every society form a whole' (Marx 1956: 123). The connectedness of these relations is pivotal to Marxism and sets the overall theory apart from other interpretations of the world. It is, in short, a theory founded in dialectics and in dialectical materialism. Marx's method is defined as 'materialistic, because it proceeds from existence to consciousness, not the other way around. Marx's method is dialectic, because it regards nature and society as they evolve, and evolution itself as the constant struggle of conflicting forces' (Trotsky 2006: 4). The strength of Marxism lies in such a formulation, marked by an understanding of the interconnectedness of often contradictory elements.

Contradiction is an oft-used expression in the Marxian lexicon and was central to Marx's understanding of capitalist development. It is a concept that at once explains and underlines many of the differences between materialist and non-Marxist interpretations and methodologies. Marx, in *Theories of Surplus Value*, distilled much of this theory when describing:

The apologetic phrases used to deny crises are important in so far as they always prove the opposite of what they are meant to prove. In order to deny crises, they assert unity where there is conflict and contradiction. They are therefore important in so far as one can say they prove that there would be no crises if the contradictions which they have erased in their imagination, did not exist in fact. But in reality crises exist because these contradictions exist. Every reason which they put forward against crisis is an exorcised contradiction, and, therefore, a real contradiction, which can cause crises. The desire to convince oneself of the non-existence of contradictions, is at the same time the expression of a pious wish that the contradictions, which are really present, *should not* exist (Marx 1968: 518, emphasis in the original).

The term contradiction is so frequently used in conjunction with crisis as to make the two virtually synonymous. Marx's comment that crises exist because contradictions exist might seem an obvious, almost banal observation. At the same time, we need to remember that capitalism exists within a world that is dominated by crisis and that crisis acts as an impetus for capitalist development, without resolving the contradictions that precipitate crisis. A seemingly unbreakable cycle exists.

Marxist theory places an obvious emphasis on *the crisis of capitalism*. The tendency for the rate of profit to fall is one of the key elements of Marxist theory and one of the most hotly contested. It is also central to appreciating this tendency to crisis. Profit derives from the labour of those who produce the goods that are sold. This is defined as surplus value. There is no single commodity that is not the result of labour or surplus value. Marx maintained and observed that in the quest for profit and increased rates of profit, the manufacturer must engage with technological innovation. This logically leads to a more efficient means of production and a greater output per unit of investment. This same technological innovation necessarily replaces people with machines. The profit rate then increases, but profit, it must be remembered, flows from labour. The less labour, the less long-term profit. It was and remains a paradox. Profits fell, not because of poor productivity, but because of increasing productivity, made possible by bigger and ever bigger investment in equipment and materials. As Rosa Luxemburg so aptly phrased it, 'In the "unhindered" advance of capitalist production lurks a threat to capitalism that is much graver than crises. It is the threat of the constant fall of the rate of profit, resulting not from the contradiction between production and exchange, but from the growth of the productivity of labor itself' (1982:34).

Other elements of capitalist crisis include the concentration of capital, the growth of the working class, a tendency towards under-consumption (or over-production) and the development and influence of finance capitalism. Overshadowing all of these is the final and most omnipresent contradiction that exists between an increasingly integrated and globalised capitalism, and capitalism's continued need and reliance on the nation-state as an organisational structure. Analysis of these features and of their inter-relationships allows for an understanding and a rational response to the contradictions in capitalist globalisation. A central and key component in this analytical tool kit is historical materialism. Scott Solomon and Mark Rupert's assertion that historical materialism 'approaches the question of globalization not with puzzlement over dramatic changes in forms of accumulation, but fully expecting them' (2002: 284) is hardly hyperbolic but simply a statement of a truth.

Marxist philosophy and theory emphasise the interaction between social classes, changes in material conditions, how society is organised and of the primacy of economic factors over political ones as engines for change. Marx interpreted how society, class relations and economic questions manifest themselves:

> In the social production which men carry on they enter into definite relations, that are indispensable and independent of their will; these relations of production correspond to a definite stage of development of their material powers of production...It is not the consciousness of men that determines their existence, but, on the contrary, their social existence determines their consciousness (1918: 11-12).

Marxism, then, unites the elements of historical materialism, economic theory and the class nature of society. Such a synthesis serves as an analytical tool to explain and interpret capitalist relations. It can similarly be used to explain and interpret Marxism and the dissension that has so long accompanied it. This materialist approach provides the basis of what Marxists declared to be a scientific analytical outlook.

Yes, it is science and yes, it matters

Is Marxism 'scientific'? For a classical Marxist the answer is obviously yes, and it most definitely does matter. To be perfectly fair, very few Marxists would disagree. It is almost a profession of faith despite the deep irony that quickly becomes apparent. The decades of crisis in Marxist theory, to put it bluntly, reflect a rejection of that very scientific method. Issues of relativism, impressionist views of society, of reacting to events rather than offering leadership are not only alive, but are disagreeably 'well' in much of contemporary Marxist theory. It is sometimes necessary to take a backward glance to better get one's bearings. Lenin (1977a) offers a clear outline of Marx's contributions to the study of historical materialism, his economic theories and the issues surrounding classes in society. These interrelated elements form the basis of Marxist theory and its claim to the status of science. First among these – ground zero if you like – is the concept of historical materialism. Intimately related to this is the fundamental premise that economic issues drive political and societal responses, that class and class conflict remain central to understanding societal developments and that a materialist construction understands historical processes as being impelled by antagonistic relationships between classes.

Historical materialism has been traditionally presented as validating the claim that Marxism constitutes a scientific method of analysis. Such validation is more than simply an exercise in semantics. If Marxism is to count for anything and if its analytical capacities are to be considered as important, then the theory needs to 'stack up'. In outlining the essential propositions that designate historical materialism and its claim to be a scientifically valid means of interpreting the world, Engels argued that:

> The materialist conception of history starts from the proposition that the production of the means to support human life and, next to production, the exchange of things produced, is the basis of all social structure; that in every society that has appeared in history, the manner in which wealth is distributed and society divided into classes or orders is dependent upon what is produced, how it is produced, and how the products are exchanged. From this point of view, the final causes of all social changes and political revolutions are to be sought, not in men's brains, not in men's better insights into eternal truth and justice, but in changes in the modes of production and exchange (1966: 50).

It was a construction that framed Marxist theory and one which has evoked wide disputation. It might be unkind to infer that careers grew and thrived, depending on the stridency of the denunciations of Marxism's claim to the status of science, but it certainly did no harm to philosophers such as Karl Popper, whose critique of Marxism has been lauded as something of a seminal work. Popper was an ardent critic of what he termed historicism as being 'an approach to the social sciences which assumes that historical prediction is their principal aim, and which assumes that this aim is attainable by discovering the "rhythms" or the "patterns", the "laws" or the "trends" that underlie the evolution of history' (1985: 290, emphasis in the original).

Popper was hardly the first and it is unlikely that he will be the last to 'prove' that Marxism is not science but rather pseudo-science. There is, after all, an almost unhealthy obsession with proving Marx to be wrong. Ernst Bloch, for instance, writing in the 1950s, sought to breathe life back into a utopian vision that attempted to lay claim to being Marxist, while totally disregarding what Marx had said a century earlier on the question of utopian thinking. Bloch contended that the emphasis on science, so central to Marxism, was a limiting feature, as was the emphasis that Marx placed on the primacy of economic factors.

Popper's propositions rejected the scientific claim of Marxism, but from a slightly different angle. To give him credit he did accept that Marxism identifies trends and tendencies that occur in social change and that these trends can neither be questioned or denied. However, Popper argued that 'trends' are not 'laws', in language that strongly echoed Eduard Bernstein's earlier work. Science, in Bernstein's estimation, was based on experience, while socialism's focus was on a future social system which, by definition, could not have an experiential basis. It is a view that was rigorously contested by Georgi Plekhanov (1976: 33) who, in the first years of the twentieth century, asserted that it was eminently realistic to suppose that a scientific study of the present allows an opportunity to 'foresee', with some degree of accuracy, what is likely to occur in the future. This, he maintained, was not the province of prophecy, or of arbitrary declarations, but on the basis of experience and the accumulation of knowledge.

The important thing for this discussion is that historical materialism can explain social transformation by identifying the dialectical interactions between productive forces and the essentially social relationship that exists in that production. The often-misleading term 'predictability' has come to represent, at least in the minds of some critics, a form of 'prophecy' rather than a conscious act of political perspective that can interpret events in a multi-faceted manner in order to make justifiable propositions.

The question of whether Marxism can be designated as science or a pseudo-science remains irritatingly vexed. The determination of Marxism as scientific came from Engels in what was essentially a critique of 'utopian socialism'. Nature, as Engels asserted:

> is the proof of dialectics, and it must be said for modern science that it has furnished this proof with very rich materials increasing daily, and thus has shown that, in the last resort, Nature works dialectically and not metaphysically; that she does not move in the eternal oneness of a perpetually recurring circle, but goes through a real historical evolution (1966: 45).

The dialectical process is one which sees opposite forces in interaction with one another, resulting in qualitative change. The simplest description of this process is the interaction of water and heat and the transformation into steam. The coming together of the two opposing forces creates a new, different substance. Engels in *The Dialectics of Nature* (1976) described dialectics as the unity and conflict of opposites and that by their interaction, quantitative changes develop into qualitative changes.

Like most issues emanating from Marxist theory, the concept of dialectical materialism has become the source of conjecture and disputation. This stems in part from theoretical divergences that result from the Stalinisation of Marxism. For many theorists it was a problem rooted in the fact that dialectical materialism became synonymous with the USSR and 'official' Soviet theory. Engels' application of dialectical materialism to the realm of natural phenomena became a problem. Controversy is never far from Marxism. This 'controversy,' for want of a better word, about dialectical materialism was and remains nonsensical, although this may be regarded by some as being controversial. A difference between Marx and Engels was confected. Marx based his consideration of dialectics at the level of social reality (human interactions), while Engels made the point that 'man' as a social object is, in essence, subject to universal 'laws' of material nature. From this, the 'reformers' and the anti-Marxist Marxists attempted to weave a net in which to catch out Engels. If it sounds a ludicrous proposition, then who am I to argue?

Whether or not Marxism is 'scientific' in its approach and outlook is not merely an exercise in semantics. It is important and is ultimately linked to the idea that Marxism and Marxists can remain optimistic without simply becoming wishful thinkers. The detractors might profit from looking at what Marx actually had to say. He was steadfast in his belief that science was far more than just a collation of facts but by necessity involved the development and propagation of theories. These theories are related to causal agents that act upon the world: entities, relations and processes. It is in the process of these theories and their actions that Marxism unites philosophical inquiry with economic analysis. This point cannot be overemphasised. At the same time, the materialist conception of history stresses the overarching importance of economics as a driver of political and societal development, but this in no way precludes Marxist theory from a deep immersion in philosophical enquiry. To arbitrarily separate the two seriously limits the theoretical underpinnings of Marxism itself. Engels (1976: 42) stressed that investigative science and theory inevitably cohere, and that theory and philosophical endeavours are intertwined. In a similar vein Albert Weisbord (1937) argued that scientific socialism originated as a method of analysis, as well as a body of conclusions, later becoming a combination of theory and practice. It becomes all but impossible to separate economic and political issues from those of philosophical considerations. In other words, ideas, like economics, exist and co-exist in historical time and space.

This co-existence of philosophy and economics in Marxist theory is perhaps best articulated when considered in relation to the core elements of class and class-based society. The class nature of society, the issue of class consciousness and the combative essence that imbued Marxism from its inception remain central to Marxist theory and to the method that Marx developed. It is precisely because of that simple fact that they remain among the most contested issues in Marxist debates.

As the capitalist crisis deepens, Marxism assumes even more importance as a means, not merely of analysis, but importantly, as an agent of change. What remains significant, and Marxists, despite all manner of differences would agree, is that 'two great discoveries, the materialistic conception of history and the revelation of the secret of capitalistic production through surplus value, we owe to Marx' (Engels 1966: 49-50). These 'discoveries' identified Marxism as scientific but remain mired in dispute and controversy. Just how Marxism became so enmeshed in crisis and confusion needs to be appreciated if Marxism is to overcome the crisis and return to a principled position that can and will offer leadership in a world bedevilled by capitalist crisis.

The crisis in Marxism

The trajectory of Marxist theory has, tragically, been towards crisis. The road to crisis has been signposted by distortions and diversions from its foundations. This foundation, and the essence of Marxism, lies in classical Marxism, based as we have already established on historical materialism as a way of understanding and interpreting the world. Marxism, as espoused by Marx, Engels, Lenin, Luxemburg and Trotsky, among others, maintained that there would be an inevitable clash of classes. This would be the result of the irreconcilable interests and antagonisms that existed. These class antagonisms could only be resolved by establishing a new economic and social order. The early promoters of Marxist theory were equally clear that this could not be achieved on the basis of individual nation-states. It was and remains a central tenet of

Marxism that socialism would replace capitalism and that this could only be successfully achieved as a world system and not confined within national borders (Marx 1974, Trotsky 2010). The twentieth century dawned. The Russian Revolution followed. It seemed that Marxist theory was being brought to fruition. The development of a world revolution was, however, not to be, and after Lenin's death Marxist theory was conscripted into the service of Stalinism and subsequently caricatured by that same Stalinism.

The Stalinisation of Marxism gave rise to a wave of theoretical responses in the period between the two world wars. It is a bitter irony that the subsequent manifestations of Marxist theory, while loudly denouncing Stalinism, have all played their part in moving theory and practice away from classical Marxist formulations. Equally ironic is the sad fact that elements of Stalinist 'theory' can be observed in contemporary Marxist theory and practice and in the institutions of the working class – the trade unions and the social-democratic parties. This is evidenced by, among other things, a reluctance to accept internationalism as central and a subsequent irrational belief in proposing national responses to increasingly global issues. The briefest exploration of some of the major trends in twentieth century Marxist thought is required.

The first significant attempt to 're-organise' Marxist theory in the post-revolutionary era came in the shape of the *Frankfurt School*. This was the forerunner of *Western Marxism,* which grew into an almost generic label of *Neo-Marxism.* The work of the Frankfurt School has been outlined and described by many scholars (Jay 1996, J Bernstein 1994, Tarr 2011). Its theorists included Lukacs (1976), whose political life was set against the Stalinisation of Marxism. Bloch (2015), another important influence, represented a trend in critical thought that promoted utopian perspectives. While consciously promoting the idea that his views were rooted within the Marxist tradition, Bloch's utopianism stood in stark contradiction to Marx and Engels' criticisms of utopian socialism. This is not to single him out for any particular or personal criticism. The work of the great majority of latter-day 'Marxist' theorists also appears to directly contradict classical Marxist positions. Herbert Marcuse, in this respect, stands as a monumental figure in presenting theory that was profoundly against Marxism. His work (1972), in both attempting a synthesis of Marxist philosophy with the work of Freud as well as in his promotion of national liberation movements (1972b) as a potential path to emancipation, saw him situated as a leading theoretician of the *'New Left'* of the 1960s.

Developments in Marxist theory and practice assumed new forms in the years following World War II. This 'Golden Age' of capitalist stability and prosperity (Glynn, Hughes, Lipietz and Singh 1990) presented new and troubling challenges for those Marxist theorists who had already made significant retreats in the name of making Marx 'relevant' to new circumstances. Marxist theory had, after all, been predicated on the idea of capitalist collapse. The apparent 'resilience of capitalism' and its capacity to overcome what seemed to be moments of existential crisis were, for many, an indication of a flaw in Marxist theory. The old verities of economic determinants, of the importance of class and of the revolutionary potential of the working class were more and more called into question. The theoretical responses were in many respects echoes of theoretical disputes that had led to the split in Marxism in the lead up to World War I. A significant and damaging result was a further distance between theory and practice.

Marcuse's (1972) *One Dimensional Man* is pivotal in some respects. It focussed on what was believed to be a decline in the capacity and potential for revolutionary change in post-World War II capitalist society and that 'individuals' rather than classes were being drawn into a system of production and consumption. It had an appeal for many and especially in a period when the immediate aspirations of the working class seemed to be met by welfare statist governments and a profitable and seemingly benign capitalism. The relative affluence of the working class in capitalist states in this period propelled many within the neo-Marxist movement to further distance themselves from the core premises of Marx and the class nature of society. This New Left ideological perspective, responding to perceived changing conditions within capitalist society, rests heavily on what it considers to be the significance that culture plays as a transformative tool. It was also deeply influenced by third-world radicalism and anti-colonial struggles. This adaptation to an anti-colonial, anti-imperialist perspective had little to do with elemental Marxist values but was regarded as a means of re-affirming a sense of relevance and building constituencies among a radicalising youth culture that was growing in Europe.

This shift in focus from Europe to third-world and anti-colonial movements found a responsive audience. Grant Farred (2000) describes how these issues rallied and radicalised student activism in the West. What was seen as a failure on the part of the 'old left', with its focus on class and particularly working-class models of struggle, led to the embracing of new forms of struggle and new arenas for activism. Frances Fox Piven (1995) sums up the feeling within contemporary Marxist thinkers that it was identity politics that provided the most fertile ground to oppose capitalism. Isaac Deutscher (1973: 68-72), on the other hand, made the obvious point that no society has effected change while relying on groups of minorities. He maintained that a stable class, rather than more transitory non-class alignments, is the only effective basis for a movement for social change. As is so often the case, that which should be obvious remains clouded by so many within contemporary Marxist circles. Non-class and supra-class approaches, that promote identity politics as a means of challenging capitalism, remain patently absurd. It remains a fact that if every issue pursued by every identity, protest movement were to be successful, the fundamental rule of capital would not be threatened.

The growing divergence in Marxist thought from its original focus on class and working-class emancipation indicates that achieving a common sense of purpose is becoming ever more difficult, if not impossible. *Post-Marxism* emerged in the late 1960s but the work of Goran Therborn as well as Ernesto Laclau and Chantal Mouffe in later decades gave prominence to this latest adaptation, if one might use such a term, of Marxist theory. The post-Marxists relegate issues of class and class struggle even further into the background. Therborn (2008), in arguing the case for post-Marxist theory, returns to issues that have become central to Marxist debates – the issue of the Russian Revolution and the effect of the collapse of the Soviet Union. This becomes important in any appraisal of Marxism and in asserting its continued relevance. This relevance, in the final analysis, can only be gauged by its capacity to unite a coherent theory with a practice that can confront, combat and replace capitalism. The crisis in Marxism may be seen to begin with the birth of the Soviet Union but was not about to end with its demise. The conditions that informed Marxist theory a century ago remain unchanged. How Marxists respond to those conditions and the crisis of capitalism remains the essential question. Therborn (2012) discusses what he sees as the passing of the 'working class century' and argues that a new era with new relationships mixing class, nation and ideology will become the focus of the challenge to capitalism. Laclau and Mouffe are quite definitive in their conceptions of the future of Marxist thought:

> Only if we renounce any epistemological prerogative based upon the ontological privileged position of a 'universal class', will it be possible to discuss the present day degree of validity of the Marxist categories...It is no longer possible to maintain the conception of subjectivity and classes elaborated

by Marxism, nor its vision of the historical course of capitalist development (2001: 2-4).

Laclau and Mouffe's renunciation of class and of Marxism's vision of the historical development of capitalism is the product of a decades-long divergence in Marxist thought. It represents a sense of demoralisation and defeatism. Marxism's central arguments are, in Laclau and Mouffe's opinion, irrelevant. Capitalism's crisis, however, has become sharper. The relevance of Marxism for the twenty-first century has frequently been called into question. This is due largely to the divergent and fragmented nature of Marxism during the past century. Wallerstein described the emergence of a 'thousand Marxisms', particularly in the post-World War II period. Marxist theory and analysis, however, remains pertinent and relevant. Such a proposition is based, in part, on the growing crisis in capitalism. None of the internal contradictions of capitalism have been resolved. Core features of Marxist theory, including the primacy of economic issues and the class nature of society, allow for renewal of a theory that is connected to practice. Marxism developed through an interchange of ideas and through often intense polemics. It remains important today to engage with contending Marxist perspectives in order to trace the trajectory of Marxist thought and to affirm Marxism's on-going relevance.

Geoff Boucher argues: 'The emancipatory social movements of the future will draw their inspiration from Marx, and Marxism, among others. This is because Marxism is a politics of mass struggle and popular mobilization in the name of a social alternative to the profit system, and this is likely to remain a feature of political life in the future' (2012: 2). Boucher's remark encapsulates much that is positive regarding the relevance of Marxism while unwittingly exposing problems within contemporary Marxism. Boucher's work, like that of Jaques Bidet and Stathis Kouvelakis (2008), among others, is valuable in outlining variants of Marxist thought and illuminating some of the disputes and philosophical discord that has been so problematic for Marxism. At the same time, Boucher takes special care not to become 'partisan' and it is here that some of the problems lie. Marxism first developed as a means of challenging capitalism and changing the world. Contemporary Marxist theory has come to focus less on Marxism as an activist ideology and more as an intellectual movement divorced from its activist roots. Despite, or possibly because of, a century of contention within Marxist theory, capitalism, while riven by irresolvable contradictions, remains unchallenged. The ideological discord and confusion in Marxism has allowed for capitalism's on-going survival.

The cycle of crisis and stabilisation that is central to capitalist development reflects a general decline in Marxism's influence throughout the twentieth century. The growth of 'official' Soviet Marxism or, more simply, Stalinism, from the 1920s played a prominent role. Karl Korsch (1931) in coining the phrase 'the crisis of Marxism' declared Marxism to be in an historical and theoretical crisis. While he correctly identified the problems within Marxism in the 1920s and 1930s, he failed to offer anything like a consistent approach to counter this 'crisis'. Declarations of the demise of Marxism are nothing new. The twentieth century heard a range of pessimistic and optimistic voices. Richard Lowenthal (1964) was by no means the first or last to write of the terminal crisis of Marxism. Lowenthal's arguments, based as they were on the divisions and disputation between 'communist' regimes, ultimately highlighted the theoretical weakness in Stalinism rather than any inherent weakness in Marxism. Michael Burawoy (1990) was among those in latter decades to defend the basic premise upon which Marxism rests. He regards the collapse of the Soviet Union as a liberating moment for Marxism. In more recent times the relevance of Marxism has been reasserted (Bidet and Kouvelakis 2008: xiv). Bidet and Kouvelakis regard Marxism as inherently adaptive while recognising that issues of class, exploitation and political domination remain central to Marxism and its relevance. The problems in re-invigorating Marxist practice, however, are real and the dislocation in theory has effectively mirrored the growing crisis of capitalism.

The range of responses to capitalist development advanced by Marxist theorists over the past century reflect the highly contested state that has long existed in Marxism. A heated contestation has significantly shaped the many paths that Marxist theory has traversed. Each adaptation to the challenges that capitalism and global political and economic realities present has served to remove the theory from a practice that aims not simply to understand but to change the world. Marxist theory became increasingly isolated and removed from class-based economics and politics, even as conditions of capitalist crisis visibly deepened. While the list of 'offenders' among Marxist theorists is an exhaustive one, they have a connecting, causal link. That link is the role played by Stalinism in the workers movement and in intellectual movements that have tried to 'prove' Marxism's relevance. This on-going role is the shadow that still hangs over Marxism in the twenty-first century. The future, however, need not be lived in the shadows.

Chapter 2

The Stalin stain

Much has been written of the bloody and bloodied history that is Stalinism. Many willing hands and minds have toiled to 'prove' an almost genealogical line of succession from Marx to Stalin. When EP Thompson (1957), the primary ideologist of the New Left, was seeking to find an intellectual wall upon which to hang his political shingle, he chose to criticise a core element of Marxist theory. This was, of itself, not surprising. There had been many before him who set about finding what was wrong with the theory. His 'lightbulb' moment was perhaps a little surprising, though, when he pointed out that Marx's base/superstructure model of economic and political development was, in fact, a 'theoretical construct' used by Stalin. The simple reality is that this 'theoretical construct' is central to Marxist theory. It was hardly a theory of Stalin's. Marxism, it has already been stressed, maintains that economics drives and informs political actions. Consequently, economic issues form a base upon which a superstructure of political interactions, the state, institutions and culture rests. Thompson was not the first and, sadly, has not been the final word in conflating Stalinism with Marxism.

Little that is good has come from this linking of what are two entirely opposed and antagonistic ideologies. Stalinist writers, theorists and apologists naturally have a purpose in making such spurious claims. For these voices there is an ideological perspective, and a spurious justification. The same cannot be said for those who, like Thompson, purport to be seeking wisdom and truth. There can be no justification under such conditions. Stephen Kotkin, for instance, in his *Stalin: Paradoxes of Power, 1878-1928*, describes Stalin as standing out 'in his uncanny fusion of zealous Marxist convictions and great-power sensibilities' (2014: xi). Stalin is also noted as advancing what Kotkin describes as 'creative Marxism' (2014: 205). What is even more breath-taking is the claim that the theory of socialism in one country somehow constituted a 'Marxist approach to geopolitics' (2014: 532). Leszek Kolakowski (2017: 284) identifies the Marxist 'roots' of Stalinism, while Mihailo Markovic answers his own ridiculous question as to the nature of Stalinism's link with Marxism, stating that there 'is no controversy about the existence of such a link' (2017: 300). The problem with such bold assertions is that there is a rather substantial 'controversy' and, it would be worth remembering, fiction ought never to be confused with fact. Many claims have been made. What we need to do is to critically examine some of these claims and move the debate to the essential politics of Stalinism.

First, we need to focus on just what Stalinism is. It is, after all, a whole lot more than the litany of crimes committed against the Bolsheviks and the working class in the Soviet Union – as horrendous as they were. Nor is it a process whereby communist parties across the world were strait-jacketed into becoming mere support mechanisms for the Soviet Union. Stalinism was, and remains, an expression of a particular world view. The theoretical basis of Stalinism, and its metastasising nature that so infected political thinking throughout the twentieth century, has long outlived Stalin. In order to finally remove the stain of Stalinism from Marxist theory, it is first necessary to appreciate what Stalinism is, how it is represented today and to recognise that it still manages to besmirch the name of Marxism.

But didn't Stalinism die with Stalin?

Marxist activists have for too many years been confronted with possibly naïve but certainly well-intentioned questions that unwittingly go to the very heart of the matter. 'You are all Marxists, all socialists. Surely you all want the same thing?' It is a question that is simple but one that requires a lot of answering.

All too often the response has been not as well-informed as it might be, and the question has rarely been dealt with effectively. While that often comes down to a lack of clarity and leadership, it ought not be a huge obstacle and especially not if we take Marxism as our starting point. There are some very salient issues in the theory that sets Marx and Marxists apart from the politics of Stalinism. One of the more significant of these is the question of whether socialism can be constructed in a single country or whether it can only be successfully built on a global scale. Classical Marxism was and remains unequivocal about this. Socialism represents the next stage in the development of economic relations. It follows and replaces capitalism. Capitalism has long since become a world system. If socialism is to replace capitalism, then it follows that it can only be as a global system. This might sound simplistic, but ever since the death of Lenin and the usurpation of power by Stalin, this simple logic has been ignored and turned on its head. What then is Stalinism's 'great' contribution to theory, and how has it proven to be so detrimental to the movement that Marxism represents?

When the issue of Stalinism is addressed in the literature, it is almost exclusively in an historical context. The theories and political programme of Stalinism are linked to the experience of the USSR. Why then is it being referred to in this work in the present tense? While it is true that there are precious few states whose political and economic existence is directly linked to Stalinism, its legacy continues to haunt and influence theory and practice today. There is a causal link between Stalinism and the crisis that has affected Marxism for the better part of a century. Attempts by successive 'Marxist' writers and theorists to 'rescue' Marxism and to make it relevant in the face of a perceived resilient capitalism have merely served to disarm Marxism. It was Stalinism that first weakened Marxism. Subsequent 'Marxists', rather than returning to Marx, 'reformed' the theory to a position whereby some can now, with a straight-face, talk of post-Marxist, Marxist theory. There is a direct link between Stalinism and the crisis in Marxism. Arguing that Stalinism is in some way an historical phenomenon is to ignore that link, to conveniently 'archive', if not 'airbrush', Stalinism from the problems Marxists face today.

The issues of past and present tense have at the same time remained since the death of Stalin. Stalinism's continued significance is linked to how political theory and action is either advanced or retarded. It has infused the working-class movement from social-democratic organisations, to the trade unions, to the great majority of political parties that proclaim socialism as their goal. Despite this, Stalinism remains a somewhat mysterious term. Literature searches and trawling the internet for meaning only confirm the thoughts of many that Stalinism and Stalin are somehow one and the same thing and consequently the 'ism' pretty much disappeared with the man. Amalgamating a range of definitions for Stalinism that appear in the literature, we come to a common definition that Stalinism represents the principles of communism associated with Joseph Stalin, characterised especially by the extreme suppression of dissident political or ideological views and the concentration of power in one person. If that sounds unsatisfactory then it is because it is profoundly unsatisfactory. Unfortunately, however, it remains, albeit synthesised, the definition that is most freely and readily available.

If we allow the 'past tense' definition to stand for just a moment, we can begin to appreciate the depth of the movement that was Stalinism and of the distortion of theory that Stalinism represents. The concept that Stalinism can be equated with the 'principles of communism' in any age might be laughable but it is a lie that has been willingly peddled for generations and one that still persists. The problem with repeating, mantra-like, an untruth, is that it becomes for many, a 'truth'. Scholars, theorists, political activists have all, at various stages, promoted this concept – that Stalinism somehow equates to Marxism.

The problem is made worse when 'reputable' figures have unconsciously, and in some cases consciously, lent their weight to the fiction. Leszek Kolakowski was by no means alone when he sought to distance Marx from what he described as 'despotic' socialism. He was just one writer who tried to conflate Stalinism with Marxism. In his case he took the extraordinary step of tying Lenin and Stalin into one tight, ideological knot, referring to 'the Leninist-Stalinist version of Marxism' (1978: 419).

EH Carr deserves a special place in this discussion. He enjoyed a long and illustrious career as a diplomat, historian, journalist and academic and was renowned as an international relations theorist. Like so many, he succumbed to the Stalin mystique. He wrote a tribute, in 1953, on the death of Stalin that was, at best, an apologia: 'In the first place, Stalin carried on the revolution in the sense in which Lenin, schooled in Marxist analysis, had conceived it…Secondly, Stalin inherited Lenin's view of politics as an "art" permitting of fairly wide opportunities of manoeuvre within the "scientific" framework of Marxist analysis' (1953: 2). Admittedly these were emotional times and his comment that 'posterity may yet learn to speak of Stalin as the great westernizer' (1953: 7) might, if one were imbued with an excessively generous spirit, be overlooked. The same cannot be said in the cold light of day. Carr, after all, had plenty of time to reflect. The question remains as to why he chose not to reflect. Twenty-five years later he was still writing paeans of praise to Stalin and his 'theoretical' acumen. Revolutions, he explained, 'however universal their pretensions and their significance, are made in a specific material environment and by men reared in a specific material tradition…the Bolshevik revolution…was also a Russian revolution and was made by Marxists who were also Russian' (1978: 4). Carr was writing of the theory that most clearly exemplifies Stalinism and most clearly sets it apart from Marxism. That theory is the theory of 'socialism in one country'.

All of this, it might be argued, is simply an historical moment. The Soviet Union is no more. A generation has been born and grown up in a 'post-Soviet' world. The theories and practice of Stalinism, it might also be argued, are simply of historical interest. Socialism, be it in one country, or as a global system, would not seem to be on the horizon. While this may be true, the fact that socialism might not be on the 'front-burner' is largely a consequence of that 'historical moment'.

Essentials of Stalinism

Carr's tributes to Stalin cut very much to the chase. He focussed on two essential elements of Stalinist philosophy and programme. The first was the theory of socialism in one country and the second an intensely nationalist perspective that came to imbue Soviet theory and practice. The 'revolution' became almost an expression of Russian nationalism. These two elements are inextricably linked and form the core of Stalinism, but they have nothing whatsoever to do with Marxism.

If we step back a little from these distortions of theory, we can easily see what the founders of Marxism felt and how they thought. There is nothing equivocal about it. Engels, in 1847, had this to say on the question of whether a revolution could be secured in a single country or whether socialism could be considered from such a perspective:

> Will it be possible for this revolution to take place in one country alone?
> No. Large-scale industry, already by creating the world market, has so linked up all the peoples of the earth, and especially the civilised peoples, that each people is dependent on what happens to another. Further, in all civilised countries large-scale industry has so levelled social development that in all these countries the bourgeoisie and the proletariat have become the two decisive classes of society and the struggle

between them the main struggle of the day. The communist revolution will therefore be no merely national one; it will be a revolution taking place simultaneously in all civilised countries, that is, at least in England, America, France and Germany. In each of these countries it will develop more quickly or more slowly according to whether the country has a more developed industry, more wealth, and a more considerable mass of productive forces. It will therefore be slowest and most difficult to carry out in Germany, quickest and easiest in England. It will also have an important effect upon the other countries of the world, and will completely change and greatly accelerate their previous manner of development. It is a worldwide revolution and will therefore be worldwide in scope (Engels 2010: 351-352).

One would think it reasonable to quote one of the founders of Marxism as a reliable source, but given the volatile and sometimes febrile nature of contemporary Marxist theory, Engels' ideas are viewed as something to be peered and poked at with mistrust. The unity of thought that existed between Marx and Engels in their lifetimes would seem to be beyond question. But no, in the eyes of some, Engels was playing some obscure game to manipulate Marx and his ideas. To what purpose, we shall leave to the tortured imaginations of these 'theorists' but Tom Rockmore, as an example, is worth contemplating, even if only in passing:

Marxism, which derives from Engels, turns on its account of the relation of Marx to Hegel, which in turn determines a view of Marx as leaving Hegel behind. I believe the Marxist view of Marx is both substantially inaccurate, and that it impedes a better view of Marx's position, including his philosophical contribution. I will be arguing that to 'recover' Marx, we need to free him as much as possible from Marxism, hence from

Engels, the first Marxist (2002: 1).

Marx, we are urged, must be 'freed' from Marxism. Engels is somehow the problem. Despite this, and other attempts at obfuscation, Marx and Marxism remains revolutionary in nature. Rockmore might try to present him as more reformer than revolutionary but in so doing is advocating 'a Marx without historical materialism, without Engels, without Marxism…a "Marx" that is not simply stood on his head, but also handcuffed and gagged' (North 2014: 360). These 'debates' go some way to showing the morass that is contemporary Marxist theory. Regardless of all of this, the thinkers to whom Marxist theory owes so much remained adamant that for socialism to succeed it needed to reflect the economic realities of a globalised economy that was already forming when *Capital* was being written.

It is to the theory of 'Socialism in one country', however, that we must return, as it remains a cornerstone of Stalinism. It effectively turned Marxist theory on its head. There may have been a logic to the theory, had it not been turned, by the Stalinist regime, into a 'central tenet' of belief. The logic can only be admitted by recognising the fact that revolutions in other countries were not immediately successful. Lenin made a series of observations on this situation, which were later 'cherry-picked' by Stalin's theorists to serve the new political realities and requirements.

The theory has come to be accepted as Stalin's, although it pre-dated the Russian Revolution by decades. German Social Democrats Georg Vollmar and Ferdinand Lassalles were the first to promote this idea (van Ree 2010). Vollmar's most significant contributions to theoretical debate in the latter decades of the nineteenth century were through his works, *On State Socialism* and *The Isolated Socialist State*. These were years of intense polemical struggle for Marxists. Vollmar's philosophical and ideological position was ultimately defeated by the forces who, only a few years later, oversaw the Russian Revolution. It is curious that his theories resurfaced, admittedly without acknowledgement, when Nicolai Bukharin presented the theory of socialism in one state to Stalin. The rest, as they say, is history or, in the unspoken vernacular of Stalinism, a falsified history.

Stalin, as has been well-documented, had a rapid change of heart on the question of building socialism in a single country. Changing one's mind is no crime but to remove records of the change of heart is something quite else. In early 1924 Stalin maintained that 'for the final victory of Socialism, *for the organisation of socialist production, the efforts of one country, particularly of such a peasant country as Russia, are insufficient.* For this the efforts of the proletarians of several advanced countries are necessary.'

'Such, on the whole, are *the characteristic features of the Leninist theory of the proletarian revolution*' (cited in Woods and Grant 2007, emphasis in the original). By the end of the year, his Foundations of Leninism had been revised and re-issued. He was now saying that 'the party always took as its starting point the idea that the victory of socialism in that country…can be accomplished with the forces of a single country' (cited in Woods and Grant 2007). Politics, of course, can sometimes be a messy affair. Things do not always run along straight lines. Sometimes, it might be argued, principles are forced to take a back seat. This might well be the subject of on-going debates and polemics. However, such a *volte face* is really quite remarkable.

To propose that the revolution could be conducted in a single country is hardly problematical. To secure state power in a single country is also well within the realms of possibility. To introduce reforms is, again, a reasonable idea, but to imagine for a second that socialism could not only be achieved, but that a classless society could be constructed, is absurd. That two diametrically opposed perspectives existed is obvious. On the one hand is the classical Marxist construction of 'permanent revolution' as advocated by Marx and Engels as early as 1850 and which was not considered an obstacle, either in theory or practice, until the Stalinisation of Marxism. On the other hand, is the Stalinist construction of building socialism in isolation from the world. Permanent revolution operates from an understanding that there is a world economy and that capitalism exists in a global setting. If socialism is to replace capitalism, then it can only be in a similarly global setting. Socialism in a single country can only be considered as an attempt to build and promote a national economy and national development.

It is in this context that Stalinism's next 'great' contribution to Marxist theory is to be found. It is in its essentially nationalist character, which again is anathema to Marxism.

Do the working people really have a country?

We live in a world beset by problems. These are made that little bit worse by the regrettable rise of economic nationalism and populism of the right and left. Let's be honest. We live in a dispirited and confused world. It is not a difficult task to prove that nationalism is not the answer, when problems have a global character, and yet the internationalism that is at the very core of Marxism is still struggling to find space in the debates that occupy the minds of so many. It is also not that difficult to draw a connection to this parlous state with the Stalinisation that made a parody of Marxist internationalism. The Stalinist regime very quickly turned an international movement into something quite else.

In 1847, the Communist League, also known as the First International, was formed. Its most famous slogan, 'proletarians of all countries unite' was clarity itself. Words are important. They have meaning. That simple slogan captured the essence of the programme of the 'League' and of subsequent Marxist parties. The International had only a brief existence, but the intent of that slogan infused the Second and, for a time, the

Third International before its destruction by Stalinism. Trotsky's Fourth International was formed as a continuer of that tradition.

There is a quote that is often attributed to Lenin. 'There are decades where nothing happens; and there are weeks where decades happen.' The history of the Marxist movement is a testament to the truth of that quote, regardless of who did say it. Marxism suffered a potentially devastating blow in the lead up to World War I. The Second International split. The great majority of Marxist parties and 'revolutionaries' chose to abandon the theoretical structures upon which their movement had rested. Instead, support was given to the war and to the various national bourgeoisies. A tiny minority 'held the line' but within a few short years a revolution had been successfully carried out and a new Third International had been formed amid a revolutionary upsurge. An intense spirit of optimism was abroad.

The Third International, or Comintern, was formed in the immediate aftermath of the Russian Revolution, but it was by no means a Russian organisation with a coterie of semi-vassal parties pledging allegiance to Moscow. On the contrary. It was a 'world party' with sections operating globally and with the aim of a global challenge to a global capitalist system. This reality was challenged and defeated after Stalin's rise to power and the demands of a 'national' form of socialism overtook the theory that had given birth to the revolution. After all, let us not forget, the Soviet Union was in the process of building socialism in one country! The revolutionary aspirations of Marxists around the world were to play second fiddle to the demands of socialism in one country. Trotsky, in the late 1920s, struggled for a return to that internationalist perspective. He wrote, in *The Third International After Lenin*, that 'in the present epoch, to a much larger extent than in the past, the national orientation of the proletariat must and can flow only from a world orientation and not vice versa. Herein lies the basic and primary difference between communist internationalism and all varieties of national socialism' (1970:1). The quote comes from a section of that book, appropriately entitled *The Program of the International Revolution or a Program of Socialism in One Country?* Later still, in 1938, Trotsky formed the Fourth International as a means of maintaining that essentially Marxist construction.

Stalinism, in a matter of a very few short years, managed to make national that which was international. Why, in the face of all this, the mast-head of the party newspaper, *Pravda*, steadfastly continued to proclaim 'proletarians of all countries unite' is one of those dark little ironies. What is perhaps darker is the shackling of intellectual and political thought that was imposed on those former 'sections' of a world Marxist party that had once been the Third International.

The rejection of internationalism in favour of a national brand of socialism was but one aspect of Stalinism and of its core value of building socialism in a single country. Stalinism was more than happy to conscript the dead to give a semblance of legitimacy to its anti-Marxist positions. In his farewell letter to the Swiss workers, in *Letters From Afar*, Lenin wrote:

> The great honour of beginning the series of revolutions caused with objective inevitability by the war has fallen to the Russian proletariat. But the idea that the Russian proletariat is the chosen revolutionary proletariat among the workers of the world is absolutely alien to us. We know full well that the proletariat of Russia is less organised, less prepared, and less class-conscious than the proletariat of other countries. It is not its special qualities but rather the special coincidence of historical circumstances that has made the proletariat of Russia for a certain, perhaps very short time, the vanguard of the revolutionary proletariat of the whole world (1932: 45-46).

It was a letter marked by optimism. It was also a letter that profoundly showed the internationalism of the Russian Marxists. To portray, as many scholars do, that there was some almost biological or genealogical link between Marx, Lenin and Stalin is to ignore such evidence. For some it was simply a matter of vacillating their way around 'inconvenient truths' and issues. Irving Howe and Lewis Coser for instance write that:

> from the party of Lenin to the party of Stalin, there is a fundamental disjuncture marked by a violent counterrevolution. To say this is not to deny that certain features were held in common by the communist movement of Lenin and the communist movement of Stalin...while Stalinism is a social and political phenomenon radically different from Leninism, it is, nonetheless, possible to find many of its sources in the theory and practice of Leninism (1962:504).

Sometimes equivocation just gets in the way.

Too much has been written trying to 'prove' links and lineages. The simple fact of the matter is that the party of world revolution that loudly called for proletarians of all countries to unite, quickly degenerated. Where once it had been based on a common programme and with national sections of the one party, it became a collection of national parties whose priority was not the promotion of revolution or of issuing an existential challenge to capitalism but rather the 'defence' of the Soviet Union. 'Stalin was, nonetheless, determined to maintain his revolutionary credentials and keep the troops, who remained diplomatic bargaining chips, mobilized. Pressure on capitalist states could facilitate Soviet foreign policy if things did not go too far...Matters were usually resolved in a conservative direction' (McIlroy and Campbell 2019: 182). The Stalinisation of the Soviet Union and of communist parties around the world was complete. Its effect on Marxist practice was enormous. Its effect on Marxist theory was just as significant.

The Comintern was, by the time of World War II, effectively redundant. The reality was that there was no 'International', and, for Stalinism, there was no need to go on with the charade. Communist parties in the rest of the world had become caricatures of the parties that had once rallied to the Marxist call to arms. Their memberships were betrayed. Marxist theorists who felt uneasy about this reality set about finding ways that might 'rescue' the theory. Herein lies the causal connection between Stalinism, the Stalinisation of the Marxist movement and the road that successive contemporary Marxist theorists have taken. It was a road that need not have been travelled. The theory, and the practice that flowed from the theory, didn't need 'rescuing' or revising, or as it turned out, jettisoning. Stalinism was the problem, not Marxism. If the Third International had become a vehicle for Stalinism and a distorted set of theories based on nationalism and national socialism, then a return to internationalism would appear to have been the most obvious course of action.

Marxism – the antithesis of Stalinism

Marxism and Stalinism stand as polar opposites. Even as Stalin was clawing his way to the top, and his 'theories' were beginning to gain an ascendancy, there were loud voices of opposition. These voices were, in an historically short period of time, silenced. The crimes of Stalinism are more than well-documented. The physical destruction of the Bolsheviks permitted the mutation of theory and, almost by definition, of a practice that might well have changed the world.

The physical liquidation of the Bolshevik party allowed for its replacement with a party of and for the bureaucracy. This, again, is well-documented and is so very much at odds with Marxist thought. It was a resistible rise and was very much resisted. A stroke, it must be remembered, prohibited Lenin from delivering a decisive blow. It was a blow that he had prepared. Upon Stalin's assumption of power, a strong 'left opposition' led by Trotsky arose. The dead, however, are many.

The 1917 Russian Revolution represented a return to the internationalism of Marxism. The split in the Second International had dealt a serious blow to this internationalist perspective, but classical Marxism had very quickly become the dominant force once more. How quickly things can change. Marxism was again in retreat. Stalinism represented all that was opposite to Marxist theory. The overarching philosophical and political premise of socialism in one country appeared to have prevailed over the Marxist proposition of permanent revolution. This 'victory' was won at great cost and the fact that the very concept of permanent revolution today sounds 'extreme' and impossible is proof of that victory. There are indeed decades where nothing happens; and there are weeks where decades happen!

The Marxist theory of permanent revolution is widely attributed to Leon Trotsky and, it must be said, his name is rightly connected with the theory. He gave intellectual flesh to the bones of this basic proposition of Marxism – that a successful assault on a global capitalism can only be possible from the standpoint of global revolutionary struggle. One country, regardless of will, cannot build an economic structure that will be superior to a global economic structure. It is a point that is so obvious that it should not have to be said.

It was not Trotsky, however, who first coined the phrase. It has existed in the lexicon of Marxist theory ever since there has been Marxist theory. Richard Day and Daniel Guido (2009), in *Witnesses to Permanent Revolution*, for instance, cite a number of occasions prior to the publication of the *Communist Manifesto* where the concept is discussed (2009: 3-4). Soon after publication of the *Manifesto* and with it the formation of the Communist League, Marx more closely articulated what was to become an accepted idea with his 'Address to the Central Committee of the

Communist League':

> While the democratic petty bourgeois want to bring the
> revolution to an end as quickly as possible, achieving at
> most the aims already mentioned, it is our interest and our
> task to make the revolution permanent until all the more or
> less propertied classes have been driven from their ruling
> positions, until the proletariat has conquered state power
> and until the association of the proletarians has progressed
> sufficiently far – not only in one country but in all the leading
> countries of the world – that competition between the
> proletarians of these countries ceases and at least the decisive
> forces of production are concentrated in the hands of the
> workers (2006).

Marxist theory was by no means a monolith and fierce debates
and polemics were waged from day one. The idea, however, that
the revolution could be anything but international and on-going
was a relatively constant theme. In 1917 Lenin commented that
'we have now reached the stage of world economy that is the
immediate stepping stone to socialism. The socialist revolution
that has begun in Russia is, therefore, only the beginning of the
world socialist revolution' (1972: 387).

It was, however, with Trotsky that the theory of permanent
revolution has become most closely identified. An extended
essay, *The Permanent Revolution* (2007), by Trotsky was first
published in 1930. It posed a direct alternative to the programme
being implemented by Stalin. It argued that capitalist states
tend to develop unevenly but that this uneven development
is simultaneously combined. By this he was highlighting the
fact that each state-based economy is increasingly bound by a
world, or global economy. From this, he was able to develop
a cohesive theory that argued against the state-based economic
developmental structures that were so much a staple of Stalinist

theory.

All of this might well be true, and it is. But, are accounts of polemical battles between long-dead protagonists not the province of historians? History can be either accessible and relevant or arid and, if not irrelevant, then without immediate import. There are precious few followers of Stalinist policies to be found today. Surely those debates have little to do with the realities and crises that face the world in the twenty-first century. While there are few who are prepared to advocate for Stalinism, there are legions of writers, thinkers and theorists who would classify themselves as 'Marxist', or more probably 'anti-capitalist'. This, too, is a truth. However, if a good idea is hard to kill, then so too is a bad idea hard to do away with. The theories and practices of Stalinism infused political thinking for decades. On the one hand, those theorists who struggled to 'rescue' Marxism from Stalinism all too frequently reformed and re-organised the theory to such an extent that little remained. On the other hand, there were those who sought to live with and around the stultifying theory imposed upon them. The Soviet Union was a fact of life. Socialism appeared to have been established in one country. It was, for many, a matter of *realpolitik*. For some, even avowed anti-Stalinists, it became a case of accommodating oneself to a reality, even if that meant entering the embrace of political opportunism.

The rifts in the Marxist movement from the time of World War I have also had a marked effect on the consciousness of many activists. That split saw a move towards social democracy and an intensely national programme. It saw a general abandonment of Marxism in favour of reformist programmes. In all capitalist states we can see similarities. Social Democrat or Labour parties dominate the thinking of many. They are associated, almost exclusively, with the economic organisations based in and around the trade unions.

Trade unions, as organisations whose existence was

predicated on fighting for the best economic interests of the working class, came to represent a symbol of struggle against capital. Such a characterisation was always erroneous and Marxist analyses of the trade unions have developed accordingly, as the deterioration of social-democratic experiences have continued. For many, including many 'Marxists', the trade unions are nascent revolutionary organisations. This flows in large part from misrepresentations, generally stemming from Stalinist theory. Marxist orthodoxy, as presented through the lens of Stalinist literature, portrayed the role of the unions not only as organisations of revolutionary potential, but as active class-conscious organisations. The work of Alexandr Lozovsky (1976) is illustrative of this tendency. The unions become, in the thinking of many, a consciously radicalised and oppositional force.

The demoralisation of practice is organically and dialectically linked to the demoralisation of theory. It is in the attempts to revise Marxism in the post-revolutionary period and throughout the twentieth century that we can appreciate the depth of the Stalin stain.

Chapter 3

A theory betrayed

Marxism was formed with the objective of combatting and replacing capitalism with something better. It maintained that the working class was a class with revolutionary potential. It was a theory that sought to act as a catalyst for fundamental change.

Marxist theory can never be regarded as immutable and unchanging. If it seeks to explain the world, as a prerequisite to changing it, then it must deal with and interact with the world as it is, and not something that can magically be ordered up to suit one's wishes. Having said that, Marxist theory – economic, political and philosophical – retains core elements. Capitalism, as the enemy of Marxism, while undoubtedly shifting and seeking to adapt to new crises, retains its own essence. It remains an indisputable fact that 'Marxists' reformed Marxism to the point of near oblivion and rendered it all but unable to lead the working class to successfully challenge capitalist rule.

The 'reformers' – the so-called 'rescuers' of Marxism – were adapting not merely to the shifts and turns of capitalism, but also to Stalinism. Stalinism was and is marked by an intensely anti-Marxist national programme. This, in turn, has an earlier manifestation and one that seriously weakened Marxism before Stalin's regime came to power and before the Russian Revolution. The deterioration and degeneration of Marxist theory begins, for us, with Eduard Bernstein's concept of the 'evolutionary road to socialism', travels through the devastations of Stalinist theory, and into a series of steps away from Marxism and its central tenets. It becomes, in the hands of contemporary Marxist thinkers, a theory divorced from its materialist roots, from its economic foundations, from an appreciation of the essential role of the working class, to a caricature and parody of Marxism. Marxism has become a theory betrayed.

This betrayal was systematic and two-edged. On the one hand there was Stalinism with its increasing hostility to Marxism. On the other hand, were those who, unwittingly for the most part, unravelled Marxist theory in order to 'save' Marxism. The trajectory of that unravelling needs to be appreciated and understood, as it is linked directly to a practice that remains leaderless, without programme or a sense of gravitas.

The crucible of crisis: reform or revolution

Whether Marxism is to fulfil its potential as that 'catalyst for fundamental change' turns on a theoretical dispute that pre-dates Stalinism, but which Stalinism echoes. That pivotal issue is the question of reform or revolution. Successive theoretical disputes and rifts can be sourced from this 'great debate'. What is to be done with capitalism and the capitalist state? How do we arrive at a just and equitable world? Can we win reforms from the state that will eventually see socialism evolve, or is it to be the revolutionary road, as Marxist theory declares? So many of the future interpretations of theory have had their roots in these polemics.

At the beginning of the twentieth century, Marxist theory was focussed on the nature of capitalism and how to respond to imperialism as a globalising force. Central to these debates were questions of revolution or reform, of whether capitalism was to be understood by breakdown theory or whether it was a self-regulating system. In the twenty-first century the nature of capitalism as a globalising force is again being debated and the 'regulatory' nature of capitalism is once again being discussed and disputed.

Capitalism's survival has been and remains for many 'Marxists' – theorists and practitioners alike – both disturbing and disheartening. The Russian Revolution failed to signal a world revolution. Revolutionary moments had come and had been defeated. Marxism was in retreat. The working-class movement in Europe had become dominated by nationalist sentiment. Social-democratic political parties won and maintained the support of the great majority of the working class. For many there appeared to be something fundamentally wrong in Marxism's optimistic view of the future. While created to expose the crisis in capitalism and to offer the necessary leadership to overthrow capitalism, Marxism itself was increasingly exposed to crisis. Despite Marx and Engels' claim that capitalism was producing its own grave-diggers, capitalism held its position of dominance and Marxism appeared unwilling or unable to present any real challenge. Viewed superficially, nothing much would appear to have changed in the decades since.

The polemics that enlivened Marxism from the late nineteenth century until the outbreak of World War I represented, at least in part, the strivings of Marxists to engage with theory in order to promote revolutionary struggle. It was also a struggle to combat ideas that were diverting the theory from its proclaimed goal of effecting revolutionary change. This reflected differences in Marxist thinking that centred on questions of reform or revolution and, almost inevitably, arose from Marxism's growth, particularly in Germany. This was due, in part, to Germany's relatively late development as a capitalist economy, the rapid rise of an industrialised working class, and the growth of social democracy. Bitter arguments ensued, as to whether revolution was the means of defeating capitalism and building socialism, or whether the path could be traversed by a series of reforms. The debate pitted the merits of revolutionary or evolutionary socialism against one another. In the 1920s Rosa Luxemburg (1982) defined the question as one of 'reform or revolution'.

Eduard Bernstein published what has been described as 'the nearest thing available to a *Communist Manifesto* of reformism' (Renton 2002: 76). First published in 1907, Bernstein's

Evolutionary Socialism (1975) did battle with both Marxist strategy and philosophy as well as criticising and dismissing the essential internationalism that underpins Marxism. He argued that the working people were increasingly becoming 'citizens' of individual nation-states with allegiances more closely aligned to the nation than to class. Bernstein's principal objective was to correct what he proclaimed to be problems with Marxist theory and philosophy. He embarked on a mission to 'revise' Marxism. The concept of revisionism has since become a pejorative term in the lexicon of Marxism. Lenin railed against the development of revisionist theories sarcastically remarking that 'there is a well-known saying that if geometrical axioms affected human interests, attempts would certainly be made to refute them... no wonder, therefore, that the Marxian doctrine, has had to fight for every step forward in the course of its life' (1977b: 49). The criticisms that came from many Marxist theorists focussed particularly on a phrase that Bernstein used to situate his philosophical position. 'To me that which is generally called the ultimate aim of socialism is nothing, but the movement is everything' (1975: 202).

The political and philosophical differences between Luxemburg and Bernstein were to inform the politics of Marxism and of social democracy for decades to come. Luxemburg, in *Reform or Revolution,* summed up the position upheld by Marxism:

> people who pronounce themselves in favour of the method of legislative reform in place and in contradistinction to the conquest of political power and social revolution, do not really choose a more tranquil, calmer and slower road to the same goal, but a different goal. Instead of taking a stand for the establishment of a new society they take a stand for surface modifications of the old society. If we follow the political conceptions of revisionism, we arrive at the same

conclusion that is reached when we follow the economic theories of revisionism. Our program becomes not the realisation of socialism, but the reform of capitalism; not the suppression of the wage labour system but the diminution of exploitation, that is, the suppression of the abuses of capitalism instead of suppression of capitalism itself (1982: 49-50, emphasis in the original).

The split in the Second International, early in World War I, saw those parties who supported a reformist path and an alignment with their own national bourgeoisies move rapidly away from Marxist theories. The essentially national programmes that they adopted sat, not uncomfortably, with the thinking of the soon to emerge Stalinism of the post-revolutionary period in Russia.

Despite the depth of feeling that surrounded these debates, it was the economic analyses of Bernstein that possibly proved to be the most controversial. The argument centred on the question of whether capitalism was a self-regulating system or prone to economic breakdown. Luxemburg referred specifically to Bernstein's premise that capitalism was unlikely to move into a general decline due to its capacity to adapt to changing conditions. This presented a major departure from Marxist orthodoxy and would, over time, come to differentiate Marxist from social-democratic theories of social change. Bernstein sought to:

demonstrate the possibility of the 'self-regulation' of capitalism. Cartels, credit, the improved system of communications, the rise of the working class, insofar as they act to eliminate or at least mitigate the internal contradictions of the capitalist economy, hindering their development and aggravation, ensure for the system the possibility of unlimited survival (Colletti 1974: 54).

It was a contention that Luxemburg rigorously rejected. She argued that Bernstein was presenting an idealist perspective whereby the, 'objective necessity of socialism, as the result of the material development of society, falls to the ground' (1982: 13). Capitalism's real or perceived capacity for self-regulation, and for reform to render revolutionary paths to socialism obsolete, became an axis around which Marxist and social-democrat polemics would rage.

This divergence in theoretical trajectory also underpins on-going disputes within Marxism. Capitalism appears to be remarkably resilient and adaptable. It was and is clearly beset by cycles of crisis and stability and yet its status as economic and socio-political paradigm has remained unassailed. This has remained a source of challenge for Marxists. The Bernstein-Luxemburg disputation over whether capitalism has the capacity for self-regulation is a case in point.

A revival of this idea of the self-regulation of capitalism occurred throughout the latter decades of the twentieth century and into the twenty-first. Regulation theory maintains that it is possible to overcome more 'mechanistic' explanations of capitalist development. The central thesis is that an explanation of capitalism's tendency to crisis and stabilisation lies in capitalism's 'requirement' of a degree of regulation. Capitalism operates, according to the theory, through cyclical, self-regulating crises. These crises further exacerbate the contradictions within the system. Capitalism reproduces and renews itself through these cyclical crises that lead, over time, to a structural crisis. This in turn creates an unregulated system which must be resolved, and a new regulated capitalist mode is constructed. And so, it is argued, the circle is complete! Michel Husson cites Alain Lipietz's commentary that 'one is a regulationist as soon as one asks why there are relatively stable structures when, given that they are contradictory, logically they should disintegrate' (2008: 178). Such observations are echoes of earlier debates within Marxism and especially between Bernstein and Luxemburg regarding the capacity for capitalism to adapt or to break down.

The regulationists consciously reject the Marxist analysis of capitalist breakdown, but still seek to distance themselves from an overtly reformist position. They have sought a 'middle' way between revolutionary socialism and reformist social democracy. Husson (2008: 187-188) contends that Regulation theory has, in recent years, moved further from its Marxist roots, and it now argues, amongst other things, for new forms of wage earning through worker share-holdings and a range of profit-sharing compromises with employers. All of this is a far cry from Marxism's call to arms but is indicative of where the reformers have taken the theory.

Theory in retreat: the period between the wars

The debates between Luxemburg and Bernstein reverberated long after the protagonists had exited the stage. They can, in a great many ways, be seen as forming a base upon which the later rifts in theory rest. The roots of Stalinism's national programme, and its deformation of theory, can, in large part, be traced to the distortion of Bernsteinian ideas and the split in the Marxist movement at the time of World War I.

The years following World War I brought not the end of capitalism, but rather, a continuation of crisis for Marxism. The Second International had collapsed and an irretrievable rift between social democracy and Marxism dominated theory and practice. The Russian Revolution and the beginning of the Third International gave an impetus for Marxism, but that optimism quickly evaporated. For many it seemed logical that there needed to be a re-evaluation of Marxist thought and practice. The revolutionary upsurge in Europe had been defeated. Stalinism became the predominant force. Flowing from that very Stalinisation came a stultification of Marxist thought, the promotion of the theory of socialism in one country, and the subsuming and co-option of the international Marxist movement into the service of Stalinist policies.

Martin Jay (1996: 3-4) describes one consequence of the Russian Revolution that would come to play a significant role in the development of Western Marxism. The Revolution moved the political centre of gravity eastward. He argues that the Marxist intelligentsia, and particularly in Germany, saw three possible responses. These were either to support Moscow's leadership and that of the Third International, back the non-revolutionary socialist movement in Germany, or pursue a complete re-examination of Marxist theory as a precursor to future actions. Significantly for the coming developments in contemporary Marxism, the fore-runners of Western Marxism chose to follow the latter path. Those future 'actions' remain ephemerally in 'the future'.

The dilemma that these 'Marxists' faced was complicated by the disintegration of the Marxist movement in Europe that came with the failure of revolutionary moments immediately after the Russian Revolution and World War I. The apparent victory of nationalism over internationalism that the Second International's collapse signalled is reflected in the development of Western Marxism. Perry Anderson (1979: 94) caustically, but aptly, asserts that Western Marxism was ultimately more 'Western' than Marxist. Anderson argues that historical materialism, as the base upon which Marxist theory is built, is only fully valid and able to exercise its full powers if 'it is free from parochialism, of any kind. It has yet to recover them' (1979: 94). Anderson's comment, while indicating the errors inherent in 'regionalising' Marxism, appears to be assuming that contemporary Marxist theory somehow 'becomes' Marxism. This is hardly an exercise in either dialectics or historical materialism. In his assumption, he seriously underestimates the very theory he purports to represent.

The years between the wars were troubled ones for Marxist theory. Understandably, Marxists such as Karl Korsch (1931) sought to wage a struggle against what they saw as a degeneration of Marxist theory and practice. It was Korsch who first introduced the idea of there being a crisis in Marxism. He was critical of the German Communist Party's perceived ideological weakness that played a significant role in the failure of the German revolution. His position drifted over time from an alliance with Trotsky's 'Left Opposition' as a means of reviving Marxism's fortunes, to his later theses arguing that:

> today, all attempts to re-establish the Marxist doctrine as a whole in its original function as a theory of the working classes social revolution are reactionary utopias...Marx is today only one among the numerous precursors, founders and developers of the socialist movement of the working class. No less important are the so-called Utopian Socialists from Thomas More to the present (1950).

Such a trajectory, during the turbulent years between the wars, was not uncommon. Anderson (1979: 24) refers to a mutation of ideas that came to be known as Western Marxism in which an 'altered universe' within Marxist theory became more and more apparent. The ramifications of this have been considerable. In particular, a separation of theory from practice became ever more apparent, as the working class in Europe became more closely identified with the politics and economics of social democracy.

There is a certain irony here, given that three of Western Marxism's most prominent thinkers (Korsch, Lukacs and Gramsci) were leading figures of the revolutionary upsurge after World War I. What transpired was the beginning of a movement that sought, consciously, to separate itself from the dialectical materialism of Engels. This attempt to 'separate' Engels from Marx is one of the more constant themes in contemporary Marxist thought. Alex Callinicos rather deftly distils much of what became the Frankfurt School and beyond, stating that 'the Frankfurt theorists refused to consider theories as merely expressions of class world-views, insisting that theoretical discourse cannot be reduced to its social conditions of production' (1983: 82). A journey that was to quickly turn Marxist theory on its head had begun.

The Frankfurt School sought to reconfigure Marxist theory to suit what it saw as the new realities of the post-war period. The defeats of the European working class and its growing accommodation to social democracy led to a shift in focus away from the working class as the axis around which change would turn. Rolf Wiggershaus argues that the leaders of the Frankfurt School did not 'put any hopes in the working class...Adorno expressly denied that the working class had any progressive role to play' (1994: 123). Another feature of Western Marxism was the removal of the classical Marxist construction that argues that the superstructure of society, political and institutional, rests upon an economic base and it is this economic base that is primary. By inverting this relationship, Western Marxism changed the emphasis and development of Marxism.

In the 1930s, Max Horkheimer (1982) further clarified the ideology of Western Marxism with his development of the concept of *Critical Theory*. Critical Theory, for Horkheimer, was a term that could be used to replace Marxism. He contended that Critical Theory (Marxism) was, in essence, a movement to abolish social injustice. It was within this theoretical framework that Ernst Bloch (2015), writing 20 years later, developed his neo-utopian vision within Marxism. Bloch's call for a return to utopian perceptions was a major departure from Marxist theory. Lenin commented on Marxism's perspective stating that Marx 'studied the birth of a new society out of the old, and the forms of the transition from the latter to the former' (1977c: 272, emphasis in the original). The utopian construct, by contrast, maintained that the 'true genesis is not at the beginning, but at the end' (Bloch 2015).

Critical Theory and the Frankfurt School dominated the thinking of radical and New Left activism after World War II. Stephen Bronner (2011) outlines how Critical Theory has 'enriched' an understanding of family, sexuality and repression, teaching practice, genocide, entertainment and literary analysis. He also states that it has added to an understanding of power imbalances, the state and global activity. This 'enrichment' in Anderson's view was in fact a reflection of a broader political defeat that had resulted in:

A remarkable range of reflections on different aspects of the culture of modern capitalism. But these were never integrated into a consistent theory of its economic development, typically remaining at a somewhat detached and specialised angle to the broader movement of society (1998: 72).

Critical Theory, as an expression of Western Marxism, sought to displace the traditions upon which Marxism had been constructed. The focus of Marxism, as outlined in Critical Theory, shifted away from the working class and class consciousness. Heinz Lubasz notes that Adorno and Horkheimer actively replaced the concept of class conflict for a theory based upon the idea of universal domination and the conflict between man and nature. Critical Theory's 'contribution' is a sleight of hand that removes the very term class from the lexicon. The 'crisis' that Korsch identified had come to full fruition and with it a distortion of Marxist theory. What was, at first, a reaction to disappointments and set-backs began a move away from classical Marxism. These 'theorists' expended considerable energies in seeking to reform, revise, re-make Marxism while effectively ignoring a force that was stultifying and deforming both theory and practice. Two fronts had opened up in the war against Marxism: Stalinism and the theorists who were unwittingly helping to disarm the theory. The *raison d'etre* of Marxism had been to both explain capitalism and to consciously act to replace it. Marxism was formed as a revolutionary movement. Lenin famously observed that 'without revolutionary theory, there can be no revolutionary movement' (1977d: 109). The years after World War I saw a flowering of theory, but it was a theory that was becoming divorced from practice. Nationalism, defeats and missed opportunities all demanded that 'old' ideas needed to be re-examined. Developing a theory for a 'new' period, however, led to the effective abandonment of the base upon which Marxism had been built. Marxist theory, from the perspective of classical Marxism, was in disarray. However, the period between the wars was marked by an intensity of questioning and debate as to the way forward. Capitalism had survived. Further strains would soon press upon Marxism with the end of World War II, capitalism's renewed strength and the dawn of a new era of capitalist prosperity.

Post-war pessimism

The end of World War II coincided with capitalism's 'golden age'. Many 'Marxists' were deeply shaken by the post-war boom and stabilisation of capitalism. The good times rolled, but for such a brief period. By the 1970s, crisis, as a natural order, had returned. The deterioration of Marxist analytical judgement spurned by Stalinism and reactions to it had paralysed contemporary Marxism, leaving it demoralised and largely ineffectual.

This 'golden age' was a period marked by economic stability and growth, an apparently contented, or at least acquiescent, working class led by social-democratic parties and a burgeoning welfare state. Cold War politics and the experience of Stalinist regimes in Eastern Europe saw Marxism further relegated, in the eyes of many, to a position of obscurity. Thoughts of a Marxist renewal, as a force to fundamentally change the economic order, appeared to be fantasy. A 'golden age' for capitalism was for many Marxist's the beginning of a new 'dark age'. Contemporary Marxism in this period again proved to be reacting to events rather than attempting to influence them. The theory became ever more defensive and remote from its core values of developing and promoting a practice that would challenge capitalism.

Two events in the mid-1950s shaped the development of Marxism in Europe. The Soviet Union's crushing of the Hungarian Revolution of 1956 coincided with the development of the New Left. Paul Blackledge (2006) argues that the New Left reformulated a democratic vision of socialism. The problem was that the New Left movement had no agreed political or theoretical agenda. EP Thompson provided the initial intellectual basis for the New Left. He sought to differentiate himself from the Marxism that had been so badly served by Stalinism. That, of itself, was no bad thing, but in his vision of a humanistic socialism, Thompson (1957) continued the shift away from Marxist truths. In criticising Marx's base/superstructure model and arguing that it was a theoretical construct used by Stalin, Thompson was, unconsciously, drawing an almost genealogical line between Marx and Stalin.

It fell to Herbert Marcuse to give 'flesh' to what was to become the basis of New Left ideology. He argued that rather than focussing on the industrialised working class, Marxists should seek to rally the broadly 'dispossessed', minority groups, unemployed and those who were yet to be integrated into the capitalist state. Capitalist development, in the post-war period, posed a dilemma for Marxism that such analysis seemed to resolve. The reality, however, lay in a somewhat different direction. The latter-day 'Marxists' were an impatient lot. A 'quick-fix' had then, as it does today, a greater appeal than conscious work and application. The relative affluence of the working class in capitalist states led many within the Marxist movement to further distance themselves from the core premises of Marx and the class nature of society. The New Left further 'adapted' Marxist theory, focussing more consciously on what was considered to be the 'transformative' role of culture. The development of the New Left also coincided with the anti-colonialist movements and third-world radicalism. Change, it was argued, was to come, not from a class-conscious workers' movement, but from largely spontaneous actions of minority groups. What emerged was the growth of identity and social movement politics.

As the old verities were being called into question, philosophical endeavours led to what has been labelled 'postmodernism'. Its largely sceptical approach to the world, and the world of ideas, had an impact on political thought and on Marxism in the latter part of the century. Callinicos (1990) asserts that postmodernism is a reflection of political frustration that stems from the disappointments of the radicalisation of the later 1960s. Central to the arguments of the postmodernists (Foucault, Derrida, Lyotard and others) is a reaction against arguments of science and reason that grew from the Enlightenment. Keith Jenkins, in describing postmodernism, claims that 'there never has been, and there never will be, any such thing as a past which is expressive of some sort of essence' (2005: 7-8). It is something of an understatement, but, in the face of such a confused set of ideas, postmodernism becomes the very antithesis of Marxism. Jean-Francois Lyotard's (1984) significant contribution to theory was that the concept of the 'grand narrative' had lost its function and its goal. This concept was further clarified by Andre Gorz (1997) when he proclaimed that seeking to find a basis of Marx's theory of the proletariat was essentially a waste of time. Theories come, and theories go. Theorists are free to espouse whatever ideas they choose. The market-place of ideas is an open one. The problem only arises when ideas, so extraordinarily at odds with Marxism, are presented as a 'development' in Marxist thought. Marxism maintains that history is a law-governed process and largely determined and driven by economic factors. It is also marked by that same 'grand narrative', particularly in relation to the working class and its role. The debate surrounding postmodernism is significant because post-Marxism's theoretical premise is so closely aligned with postmodernist theory.

Central to post-Marxist ideology is the dismissal of the 'old' politics of classical Marxism. In keeping with the intellectual scope of postmodernism, as well as the movement away from class-related political analysis, it is an appeal to the 'revolutionary potential' of identity politics and broad, non-class social movements. Fortunately, there were, and remain, voices that are raised against such perspectives. Peter Critchley (1997), for instance, argues, albeit rather guardedly, that socialist renewal is certainly possible by using Marx's analysis without discarding class forms of struggle. Critchley regards the development of post-Marxism in terms of a paralysis of the will that is required to change the world. Stuart Sim argues that post-Marxism is 'as much a symptom of a problem as a solution to the left's ills; the problem being that radical politics has become very dispersed in the last few decades' (2011: 20).

While radical politics became 'dispersed' in the post-war period, the quest to understand capitalist political economy within a Marxist framework continued. The twentieth century dawned amid capitalist crisis and unresolved contradictions. It was a century that saw wide divergences and developments in Marxist theory but with capitalism still secure. Marxism remains divided. Marxism was formed with the objective of fundamentally changing society. Its focus was the class nature of that society. Many 'Marxisms' evolved in the last century. Each of these divergent trends have built and extended theoretical positions, but with each new representation, the importance of class and working-class struggle has diminished.

An ever bleaker and more dismal horizon

Among the bleaker expressions of contemporary Marxist thinking are arguments that suggest that the movement for socialism in the twenty-first century must avoid the linking of economic and political relationships and that a key 'flaw' in Marxist analysis is its insistence that socialism represents the assumption of power by the working class (Chodos 2007:190-193). The fact is that the working class has become something of a problem for many contemporary Marxists. Gorz (1997), for instance, elaborated a theory of labour that increasingly regarded the working class as either impotent in the face of the structures of capitalism, or as representative of a privileged minority. He regarded the working class as a shrinking force that was incapable of playing a conscious role against capitalism. The issue of the working class and its role in the transformation of society has been at the centre of Marxist theory and practice. It has also been at the centre of dislocation within Marxism.

It is probably not all that surprising that recent debates within Marxism have focussed less on economics and more on philosophical questions. Marx began his professional life as a philosopher and moved resolutely to the field of economics. Western Marxism consciously developed its theory and ideological base on the philosophy of Marxism rather than its economic propositions. It was a move that saw theory shift inexorably away from the working class and the classical Marxist position that economics and economic struggle between classes is the dominant and motivating force. To arbitrarily separate the component parts of economics and philosophy can only weaken Marxist theory. Similarly, theory and practice act as an integrated whole. To separate one from the other leads to a theory that is baseless.

In seeking to renew its claim to relevance, contemporary Marxism more and more diverged from its fundamental premise of class and class struggle as a means of combatting capitalism.

However, if Marxism is to make a serious claim to relevance, then the unity of theory and practice needs to be more obviously integrated. It is thus appropriate, if only briefly, to re-visit some of the theoretical observations of Marxism and particularly in relation to issues of class and class consciousness.

Class, as a defining element in capitalist society, has long been central to Marxist analysis. Anderson (1974: 49) offers a suitable explanation of Marx's concept of class-in-itself as opposed to the state of class-for-itself which denotes a conscious and independent movement to pursue its own interests. Such a position is certainly difficult to attain but failing to reach such a position has serious consequences for the working class. The essence of class consciousness, and its possibly elusive character, is further articulated by Anderson (1974: 60-61). Two components – a radicalised intelligentsia offering an ideological leadership and a motivated working class – provide a framework within which consistent class consciousness might develop. Such a view is based on Marx's (1956: 195-197) conception of the development of class relations whereby the working class seeks to consciously promote, and struggle for, its own interests. The working class, no matter how militant it may be, remains limited in its potential if it must act within the constraints of the capitalist state from which it seeks emancipation.

Class consciousness is not simply militancy. It requires a leadership, either from within the working class or acting in concert with the working class, to advance its interests. Lenin's (1977d: 113-114) comments, that mass strike behaviour without effective and conscious leadership is but an embryonic form of class consciousness, is more acute today than ever it was. Such energy must be channelled, or it is energy too easily spent. Trotsky, describing the necessity of political leadership, remarked that 'without a guiding organisation the energy of the masses would dissipate like steam not enclosed in a piston box' (Trotsky 1965:17).

Political leadership, and the role of the working class, remains at the core of Marxism's claim to relevance. This understanding is fundamentally linked to the question of Marxism's purpose. Marxism emerged to describe and offer a critique of capitalism. This has remained its strength. Integrated with this, however, is the *purpose* of Marxism: to organise and offer leadership to the working class in its quest for emancipation. The role of the working class and the combative nature of Marxism, however, became less central to Marxist thinking in the twentieth century.

The history of Marxist thought in the past century or so has been marked by division and dislocation. Fundamental to the rifts in theory has been the question of how to deal with Stalinism. In 'dealing' with Stalinism, theory became increasingly separated from practice. The future requires a practice that is informed by theory and a theory that exists to challenge capitalism and change the world. How that will develop remains to be seen. David North, paraphrasing Marx, argues that 'we live and fight in the world of "objective conditions", which is both the source of our present-day troubles and their ultimate solution. Whatever shall emerge in the future shall be the product of conditions that exist today' (North 2014: 132).

Today there are many 'Marxisms' and yet all stem from the one intellectual base: the analysis of Marx and Engels, who presented a deep critique of capitalism and of its evolution. The purpose of this critique was not simply to analyse and to appreciate the development of capitalism, but to provide a theoretical platform that would be used to combat capitalism and to replace it. Michael Burawoy and Erik Olin Wright claim that Marxism is 'a comprehensive worldview for understanding the social world. It provides the theoretical weapons needed to attack the mystifications of capitalism and the vision needed to mobilise the masses for struggle' (2006: 462). Marxism, however, despite providing these 'weapons', has not been able to mobilise the 'masses for struggle'.

Marxism remains relevant only if it answers fundamental questions that confront the working class. These questions are inextricably linked to the potential and capacity for the working class and its allies to develop an independent consciousness that both responds to and combats capitalism and the state. As Marx famously declared, 'philosophers have only interpreted the world, in various ways; the point is to change it' (Marx and Engels 1964: 647). The world, or more specifically the economic and political structures of capitalism, has not been changed.

A rift between theory and practice has long been evident and has long plagued Marxism. Marx argued that 'it is not enough that thought should seek to actualize itself; actuality must also strive towards thought' (1977: 138). Lukacs paraphrased this, stating that only when 'consciousness stands in such a relation to reality can theory and practice be united' (1976: 2).

The theoretical shifts in Marxism have a common thread and a shared parentage. In seeking to maintain relevance in a changing world, and to distance itself from the stain of Stalinism, contemporary Marxism has become a reactive force. There is a perception among many 'Marxists' that the 'revolutionary potential' of the working class has somehow dissipated. However, the class nature of society remains a cornerstone of Marxist theory. This shift in emphasis evolved over decades. 'Marxist' theory sought to adapt to new perceptions and new challenges. Western Marxism, in the period between the wars, reacted to a political and geographical shift eastward that followed the Stalinisation of Marxist theory. It was also responding to the gathering strength of social democracy and a working class that, having been theoretically and organisationally disarmed, exhibited a weakened sense of consciousness. Capitalist stabilisation after World War II and a more acquiescent working class led many Marxists to pursue new, alternative paths in a quest for relevance. New Left activists and postmodernist, post-Marxist theorists argued new ways of engaging in struggle were required.

Marxism, despite theoretical disputation and divergence, remains a valuable vehicle for analysing and understanding capitalism and capitalist globalisation. This, of itself, is not enough. It does not necessarily promote a theory that will effect change. Marxism was created to provide analysis and critique of capitalism. Inseparable to this was its role of offering guidance and leadership in the course of combatting capitalism and of fundamentally changing economic and societal structures. How Marxism responds to the latter historical component will frame its future, its relevance and the future of capitalism. Gamble asks what sort of future does Marxism have? 'It might linger on like mediaeval scholasticism...with no observable connection to anything in the real world' (Gamble: 1999: 4). He hopes that this is not the future because 'there is an intellectual core to Marxism which is worth preserving and which is capable of further development' (1999: 4). Another question remains but is often unasked. Can Marxism not only answer the questions that modern capitalism poses, but also act as a catalyst for fundamental change? The answer to that question is determined by the practice that Marxist theory generates. Marxist theory has been betrayed. So too has the practice of Marxism. Betrayal need not be the end of the story. What then has happened to the revolutionary practice of Marxism?

Chapter 4

Into an alley, blindly

'Practice without theory is blind, theory without practice is sterile.' It is such a well-worn phrase but, sadly, an apt one when considering how the demoralisation of theory has so badly served those who would dare to confront capitalism. Marxism, we must remember, was formed and developed with a specific purpose in mind. It was not to be simply an idea and a philosophical perspective, regardless of how interesting that might be. It was a flesh and blood ideology that existed to organise a struggle against the rule of capitalism and to fundamentally change lives and the world. It was designed to be a theory that informed practice. That, after all, was the reason that the First International, the Communist League, was formed. If theory degenerates, then it can hardly be surprising that practice is affected.

Those who seek to enter into 'struggle' against capitalism, against inequality and for something better, are confronted with a capitalism that lurches from crisis to crisis, and throughout the past several decades has become caught in a contradiction of its own inevitable creation. Capitalist economic relations are globalised as never before. A growing integration of capital is a simple fact. The nation-state is, in many respects, a burden that capital no longer requires and yet desperately needs to maintain a sense of order and calm. The state is, of course, the state of and for the economic ruling class. The nation-state has an intensely difficult role to perform. Historically it engendered this sense of calm, of stability, of order. Through careful use of the ideology at its disposal, through the various institutions it was able to use, it promoted and nurtured a feeling that the 'nation' is what we have in common and this is what unites us and acts as the mortar that keeps the wall of society intact and erect. The contradiction between the need of a stable state structure and a freedom of capital to ignore borders is the contradiction that threatens capitalism, the state and the future of the world as frictions between states becomes ever more acute.

This contradiction has special meaning for those who are most negatively affected by it – the working class. Despite the nationalist rhetoric, despite the economic nationalism, despite the populist appeals, the fact remains that the relationship between capital and labour can never be anything but antagonistic. What, then, is to be done? The working class and its organisations have been incorporated, integrated and legitimised within the nation-state. This is a point frequently overlooked by many 'Marxists' who cling steadfastly to the belief that the trade unions offer a viable platform for struggle against capitalism and that, at best, a globalised capital can somehow be combatted by a globalised union movement. The central role of the working class in anti-capitalist movements has been downplayed by many contemporary Marxist theorists. This has been particularly evident since the 1960s with the rise of identity politics and the development of new forms of social movement activism. Marxist theory developed from the premise that the working class is a potentially revolutionary force because of its central wealth-creating role within capitalism. Recent iterations of Marxist theory have shifted emphasis away from the role of the working class, focussing rather on the middle class as a force for change.

Consequently, we need to consider the rise of identity politics as an attempt to oppose the negative aspects of capitalism. We also need to recognise not only the serious limitations that become immediately apparent from identity politics but the fact that capital has never been threatened by limited identity-based politics. The limiting nature of such political manifestations, and the narrow focus that they unwittingly engender, resulted in attempts to broaden these non-class political expressions of dissent. The point to bear in mind, however, is that class, for

Marxists, not only matters but is a vital piece of the puzzle.

A serious discussion of these 'new' social movements is required. They have repeatedly shown a capacity to mobilise large numbers, but also a tendency towards dissipation and retreat. This is a consequence of a limited programme, a lack of clarity in objectives, and an on-going problem of leadership. An analysis of the strengths and weaknesses of these non-class and supra-class social movements is therefore needed. These movements often engage large numbers of people, burn brightly, but burn briefly. This is due, in large part, to a lack of ideological clarity and scope. Regardless of any potential success of non-class movements, no threats to the rule of capitalism have emerged, and nor could they be expected to emerge under such conditions.

This ultimately brings us back to the question of theory and practice. This, in turn, draws our attention again to the distortions of theory that sprang from both the Stalinisation of Marxism and the retreat from classical Marxist theories that ensued in the post-revolutionary years. For too many, this has meant a deep questioning of the relevance of Marxism in the twenty-first century. Marxism remains the most appropriate vehicle to effect change. But capitalism remains unchallenged, despite the rise of anti-capitalist movements, social movements and anti-globalisation activism. It is in a unity of theory and practice, that a renewed Marxism can provide, that such a challenge can be perceived. Marxism's continued relevance is reasserted and confirmed by its capacity to project leadership that can and will confront and challenge capitalism.

First, find the real enemy

A crime has been committed. Those who seek a better future, free from capitalism and its insoluble contradictions, free from crisis and inequality, have been cast adrift. This becomes acutely obvious when observed against the backdrop of the rapidity of capitalist globalisation. There is a common fear and criticism but what is to be done?

As with all developments in capitalist relations, there are those who suffer. It is no surprise that those who suffer most are the working class. The crisis in capitalism that precipitated globalisation from the 1970s saw a dramatic change in how capital arranged its affairs. Traditionally labour was mobile, moving to where jobs could be found. Marxist theory argues that there is a tendency for profits to fall. The crisis and subsequent speed up of capitalist globalisation saw this turned on its head. Capital, and an increasingly global and integrated capital, moved to where the least expensive labour might be found. One consequence was a shattering of manufacturing in the developed countries. Another was the construction of an industrial working class in the developing world. Naturally there was ill-feeling, hostility and antagonism, but how was this to be expressed, and what outcomes might be expected?

Capitalism and globalisation have always been synonymous. Changes to capitalism have made this tendency towards globalisation more prominent and have directly led to conditions of heightened inequality. Globalisation has become a source of discontent and disquiet. Globalisation has been accompanied by accumulation of wealth and an intensification of poverty. The developed economies have seen a de-industrialisation, growing unemployment and a stagnation of wages that has led to increasing disparities between the extremely wealthy and the 'rest'. There have been, of course, many claims that globalisation has led to millions in the developing world being brought out of poverty. This may be the case, or at least it is on a superficial telling of the story. The developing world has seen and is seeing a dramatic rise in an industrial working class. This means a relatively quick rise from abject poverty to poverty. While this may be lauded the fact remains that the degree of exploitation remains and the relativities between rich and poor remain and increase.

For many, the question appeared to be, how best to resist globalisation, and how to promote an anti-globalist or anti-capitalist agenda? For some it became, and remains, a question of reversing the tendency of capitalist globalisation: to 'de-globalise'. For others, it is to present globalisation as a political issue that can be somehow separated from over-riding economic considerations. What needs to be remembered is that there is an inseparable unity between economic globalisation and capitalism. However, globalisation, in itself, is not the cause of the misery that anti-globalists depict. It is capitalism that is the ultimate source of that misery.

Among the dynamics or rather the dialectic of capitalist globalisation in the contemporary era is the relationship between the nation-state and a globalising economic reality. Paul Cammack (2003) proposes a 'new' materialist approach relating to globalised capital in the twenty-first century. He considers the implications for an emerging single capitalist system. Individual governments, he contends, share a collective interest in capital accumulation through an array of multilateral institutions. At the same time, individual states exhibit a more traditional role of seeking advantage over other states. Such a proposition highlights the contradiction of the nation-state evolving into a component of globalised capital, while still maintaining elements of national capitalism. This, while speaking most directly to changes that have taken place in capitalism, is also reminiscent of the era of imperialist rivalry when capitalism broke out from the limitations of national boundaries and onto a global stage.

This all-consuming contradiction is not hidden from view. The theorists among contemporary Marxists have considered the issues. There are self-imposed limitations upon their various analyses. For the most part, it is the problem of being unwilling or unable to break from nationalist perspectives, despite the overwhelming evidence that suggests the problems are global in nature. There are those who optimistically, almost 'headily', write of class conflict, but of a class conflict that remains rooted in the nation-state. Berch Berberoglu (2009: 47), for instance, sees capital in the US facing an imminent challenge from the American working class. It is true that the US has seen a remarkable upsurge in militant working-class responses to the devastation that has befallen them. There are embryonic moments where US workers have drawn the lessons of recent history and have sought links with their fellow workers overseas, but theorists such as Berberoglu still maintain that hard-to-shift focus that things can change within a single country.

Leslie Sklair (2002: 272-296) represents a quite different current in theorising an anti-globalisation strategy. 'Counter Movements' that include localising anti-globalisation struggles through protectionist policies, identity politics and ecological politics are presented as a means of 'challenging' globalisation. 'Slowly, labour, environmental and other movements are being drawn into the non-violent fold' (Sklair 2002: 296). Sklair is not alone in promoting protectionism. Populists of both left and right sadly come together in moments of confusion and crisis. Networks of social change are, in Manuel Castells' (2004: 428) estimation, a glimpse of a new society in an embryonic form. These views identify some of the difficulties facing the working class and its relationship both to the nation-state and to capitalist globalisation. Broad, supra-class and non-class theoretical propositions offer what appears to be an enticing potential for activism and for expressing dissent but have an equally strong potential to be diverted.

To be fair, Sklair (2000: 82-83) does acknowledge and focus on the crisis facing the working class. He accepts that a resolution to that crisis can only come from opposing global capitalism and not simply globalisation. The problem is, how might this opposition develop? In Sklair's opinion, this struggle might well unfold from the development of social movement politics and an appeal to a broadly defined 'democratisation' of global society. How society is to be 'democratised' is another question and one rarely discussed seriously by the theorists of the later twentieth and early twenty-first centuries.

We live in an age where 'Marxist' theory has had a negative impact on practice, and where the working class has effectively been relegated, at best, to the background. The importance of class has been downplayed and a sense of despair stalks the earth. Spontaneity and the 'quick-fix' become important. Many opponents of globalisation, and of capitalism, have pointed to the magnitude of the global response to the excesses of capitalist globalisation. They argue that the protests at the World Trade Organisation (WTO) meeting in Seattle in 1999, and the creation of the World Social Forum in 2001, the 'Occupy Wall Street' movement and the like are indicators of a global resistance movement that might challenge capitalist globalisation. William Robinson (2004: 168-172) describes the chronology of events, of the rise of this anti-globalist movement and of a lack of strategy in the opposition movement that led to its failure. The divergence of ideas and of proposed outcomes from such an amorphous grouping was, and remains, an unavoidable obstacle. Eclectic coalitions ranging from anarchists to socialists, from broadly anti-capitalist activists, to democracy advocates and green groups formed and dispersed. What united these disparate groupings was their belief that globalisation could either be controlled and countered or reversed. The coalitions came, and the coalitions went. They shared a belief in what they were against but not what they were for. They shared no programme, offered no leadership and all too often left little by which to remember them. The tendency towards spontaneity led to what was almost inevitably a downward trajectory within the anti-globalisation movement.

To suppose, even for a moment, that globalisation, while undoubtedly linked to the rise in inequality in the world, can be regarded as having a progressive component inevitably invites criticism. However, such a perspective can be defended. Marx's construction of an historical materialist conception of history, as Susan Jellissen and Fred Gottheil (2009) contend, leaves little doubt that globalisation is an inevitable process. Marx's description (Marx and Engels 1975: 195-201) of the significance of the introduction of steam and of the railways in relation to the transformation of India has often been used to indicate an almost globalising 'mission' of capitalism, and yet Marx was implacably hostile to capitalism as it represented an intensely exploitative system. The vision of a globalised world economy was, in Marx's estimation, a step towards an economic and political formation that would replace capitalism. It would only be replaced by recognising the class nature of society and consciously seeking to advance class struggle. Marx, subsequent Marxists, and particularly classical Marxists have sought to develop that consciousness as an integral element in changing and challenging an ever-globalising capitalism.

What to do with the working class?

Capitalist globalisation, as an expression of changes in capitalism, has obvious and direct implications for the working class. Capitalism has long moved away from any restrictions imposed by national boundaries. Marx declared that the working people have no country. The same slogan applies equally to capital. The industrial working class formed and grew as national capitalism developed. Working class organisations, both economic and political, were framed by this reality. The relationship between labour and capital, central to Marxist theory, is an antagonistic one, affected by irreconcilable class interests.

Such observations ought to be obvious and yet far too many theorists of contemporary Marxism have largely dismissed the working class. Stalinism talked of the working class but set serious limits as to how that class might respond to capitalism and dismissed the internationalism of that class. Those who either consciously or unconsciously remain in the nationalist snare that Stalinism set still pay lip-service to the working class, or at least to the trade unions. Many latter-day theorists have gone a step further. They have sought to airbrush the working class away and still effectively dismiss internationalism. There is much talk of 'anti-capitalist' movements and of 'resistance' to capitalism and globalisation, but without the working class as a key player, it is so much empty chatter.

Any analysis of 'anti-capitalist' movements, or of potential challenges to capitalism, needs to consider the working class and its organisations. To defend and strengthen their position, workers historically organised themselves at the point of production. Economic and political alliances of the working class were resisted by the ruling class, often violently, but over time these manifestations of working-class consciousness were increasingly incorporated into the mechanisms and structures of the nation-state. The trade unions were tolerated, legalised, legitimised and evolved into essential components of the state. So too with political parties of the working class and especially social-democratic political parties.

A consequence of this integration appears to answer Luxemburg's famous question of whether the working-class movement should adopt a 'reform or revolution' approach. Marxist views of a revolutionary path to emancipation became a minority perspective. Reformist ideology became dominant, but in the twenty-first century, neither reform nor revolution appear on the agenda of the leadership of working-class organisations.

The primary organisations of the working class have long been social-democratic political parties and the trade unions. However, when the term working class is permitted entry into the debate, it is invariably the trade unions that become the focus. Most activists who still place any importance on the working class hold fast to a belief that the trade unions are capable of far more than reality has ever allowed. A mystique has grown over time, but it needs to be questioned.

Marxist attitudes to the unions have shifted as the capitalist state has developed. Richard Hyman (1975) identifies a range of Marxist interpretations, from the optimistic view of the early writings of Marx, to the more pessimistic position adopted by Engels and Marx's later work, as well as those of Lenin and Trotsky. Marx's early work (1956: 150-151) saw a potential for unions to play a major role in the overthrow of capitalism. Engels (1984) also regarded the union movement as a powerful force for change. Marx (1986a: 226) also warned the working class that it was confronting the *effects* of oppression and not the *cause*, which was capitalism. Lenin (1977d), responding to the issue of 'economism' in the working-class movement, pointed out that unions are not and cannot be a threat to capitalist rule precisely because the unions had effectively been incorporated into the state. Trotsky took this analysis a step further when he wrote of 'the degeneration of modern trade union organisations in the entire world...drawing closely to and growing together with the state power' (1972: 5).

Classical Marxism has recognised this tendency towards a growing accommodation with the state. Despite this, political activists and theoreticians, often from within the Marxist tradition, maintain that trade union activity is an effective path towards resistance to capitalism and even a consciously radicalised and oppositional force. Some go so far as to argue that the working class can best respond to capitalist globalisation by developing transnational union organisations. Such views give working class organisations an independence that is, to be kind, largely imaginary.

The capacity of the working class to develop an independent class consciousness is, in Antonio Gramsci's estimation, limited by the hegemony enjoyed by the ruling class. He described the actions of the state as 'the entire complex of practical and theoretical activities with which the ruling class not only justifies and maintains its dominance but manages to win the active consent of those over whom it rules' (Gramsci 1971: 244). The ability to engage in defensive struggle, let alone to promote an independent offensive against the capitalist state, has further diminished since the explosion of capitalist globalisation in the 1970s. Peter Leisink (1999: 19) cites International Labour Organisation (ILO) figures from the *World Labour Report* of 1997-98 to show a general decline in union membership. Later statistical research from the ILO (2008, 2015 and OECD 2014) indicates that this tendency has only worsened.

'Marxist' theorists sprang into action to 'discover' what was going on. Some see the problem as being a bureaucratisation of the unions. Others glibly put it down to the strength of global neoliberalism. Still others blame the loss of union membership on a weakening of social-democratic and other 'left' parties, while another 'explanation' is that the capacity to manage labour relations has been moved from the state to globally-based capitalist corporations. Like so many things, each proposition carries a kernel of truth, but that very integration and co-option of working-class organisations into the mechanism of the state ensures that the present looks bleak and the future even more so.

Despite this, the working class in so many western states has shown a growing sense of awareness and militancy. Resistance is, after all, the inevitable outcome of a class-based society and of capitalist state rule. Leadership, or rather its absence, is a determining factor in the success or failure of that resistance. Another factor is the end result to which such resistance aspires. For some (Yates 2003: 236-237) it becomes crucially important that trade union leaderships should respond, not merely to traditional structures and issues, but that they 'adapt' to accommodate a diversity of needs within their unions. Barry Gills and Kevin Gray (2012) describe what they see as an upsurge of revolt in the form of 'people power' in the face of the assault of globalisation. Joel Rocamora (2012) enthusiastically promotes the view that what effectively remain largely spontaneous actions can achieve lasting results and that uprisings are inevitable because capitalism continues to produce victims. While a range of perspectives might be evident regarding questions of labour leadership, it remains clear that with integration into the state, the working class has become increasingly less well equipped to engage in independent struggle for emancipation. Barrington Moore Jr (1978: 472-475) critically explores perspectives on working-class responses to the growth of capitalism. He describes a tendency towards acquiescence and integration leading to a reduction in ideological struggle. You might think that he might be able to connect a few dots at this point, but no. He is, at the same time, highly critical of the Marxist concept of developing class consciousness. Issues surrounding class consciousness are inextricably linked to leadership and elements of confusion surrounding what is and is not class consciousness.

Kees van der Pijl (2002: 142) writes that while every ruling class claims 'universality' for itself, the reality is that social conflict is what marks out all class-based societies. Social conflict, while an inevitable part of class society, should not, however, be confused with the development of class consciousness. John Koo (2000) notes that a sense of growing union identity, and even a strengthening of union influence and militancy, does not necessarily indicate class consciousness. Michael Mann (1973) identifies a hierarchy of class consciousness ranging from identification with the class, to recognition of capitalism as an antagonistic opponent, to finally accepting a goal to be attained through struggle.

Issues of leadership, of capacity, of vision, are all central to the over-riding question, not merely of resistance to, but also eventual emancipation from capitalist state structures. Lenin's (1977d: 113-114) assessment that strike action is but an embryonic form of class consciousness is worth repeating in this context. The problems associated with spontaneity as opposed to consciously constructed actions remain valid today.

Perhaps 'identity' will solve the problem

The working class, it seems, is a bit too much like hard work for many 'anti-capitalist' warriors. For many activists, this is almost understandable. After all the theory upon which their practice rests has been resolutely down-playing the role of the working class for decades. Still, as the saying goes, when one door closes, another opens. Exit class-based theory and practice, stage left and enter identity politics. The growth of identity politics highlights an important aspect of the ideological dilemma faced by Marxism since the 1960s and the development of New Left politics.

Identity politics came to prominence in the 1970s. This followed the heightened radicalism of the late 1960s. The 'left' and many in the divergent 'Marxist' movement were seeking a route to relevance. The 'revolutionary potential' of the working class had been disputed and apparently discredited, or at least in the eyes of these same theorists. The politics of identity seemed to offer a new hope and filled the vacuum rather nicely. Manuel Castells makes the obvious point that 'identity is people's source of meaning and experience' (2004: 6). To seek identity, to belong, in the face of an intensely alienating society cannot be discounted and especially so as capitalist globalisation is presented as destructive of identity and autonomy. A deepening sense of alienation is there for all to see. Marx in his *Economic and Philosophic Manuscripts of 1844* outlined this process of alienation so inherently a part of capitalist relations:

What constitutes the alienation of labour? First, the fact that labour is external to the worker, i.e., it does not belong to his essential being...The worker therefore only feels himself outside his work, and in his work feels outside himself...

His labour is therefore not voluntary, but coerced; it is forced labour. It is therefore not the satisfaction of a need; it is merely a means for satisfying needs external to it...the external character of labour for the worker appears in the fact that it is not his own but someone else's...it is the loss of self (1969a: 110-111).

The working class under such conditions is inevitably estranged, not just by capitalist relations but from capitalist society and from the state itself. The middle class, too, is more and more affected by this sense of alienation.

Castells, in clothing identity politics in suitable intellectual garb, argues that identity assumes a political character and is portrayed as a means of rallying like-minded individuals, as well as presenting a means of combatting the 'institutions' of society that form the basis of oppression (Castells 2004: 8). Incidentally he also argues that working-class decline can be partially attributed to the rise of identity politics in the 1960s and 1970s and that the working class can no longer be regarded as the primary actor that will precipitate change. The logic of such an argument is, at best, tortured.

Regardless of problems of logic, the fact remains that the politics of identity became more influential as the politics of class declined. The 1970s saw a dramatic rise in political movements based on race, ethnicity, gender and sexuality. Those who seek to legitimise identity politics as saviour are forced to engage in circular arguments that do not really hold up to scrutiny. Frances Fox Piven (1995), for instance, argues that the expansion of capitalism and its globalising character has acted to weaken and destroy the more traditional working-class politics of resistance. Globalisation, in such a construction, was the catalyst for the rise of racial, ethnic, religious and gender conflicts, with identity politics as the inevitable consequence. Piven makes two contradictory claims. Identity politics at once 'makes people susceptible to the appeals of modern nationalism, to the bloody idea of loyalty to state and flag, which is surely one of the more murderous ideas to beset humankind' (1995: 105). He simultaneously describes the politics of identity as 'a potentially liberating and even equalizing development, especially among subordinate groups, and the more so in a political culture already dominated by identity politics' (Piven 1995: 106). In other words, identity politics is particularly useful when identity politics already exists.

Feminist politics, and particularly the debates around patriarchy, have fuelled the growth in identity politics. Caroline Pateman (1988) argues that patriarchy long pre-dates capitalist oppression, and that the relationship of sexual domination is a separate oppressive structure to that of capitalism. She rejects the notion that individuals 'freely' engage in property exchange or, more significantly, in the sale of labour power. This is true to an extent. There is more coercion than freedom. Pateman's view is that such a conception is a 'fiction' that masks patriarchal domination. A more satisfactory argument is that with the division of labour, and with the emergence of class-based societies, patriarchal organisation dominated. Capitalism, as it developed, simply used that which was already the norm (see Engels, *Condition of the Working Class in England* 1984 and *Origin of the Family, Private Property and the State* 1986). Yes, patriarchy is deeply rooted in society and yes, it is older than capitalism. Whether it is 'more fundamentally oppressive than capitalism' as some maintain is a debatable issue. It is capitalism that remains the central issue and problem. Capitalism's use of ideology to promote illusions that patriarchy, or race, or ethnicity, are separate issues and detached from capital itself allow it to maintain divisions among people.

This is equally true in relation to what is an issue of immediate and existential importance – the issue of environmental destruction and climate change. Arne Naes (1973) advanced the concept of 'ecophilosophy' as an expression of 'deep ecology'. He argued that both exploiter and exploited are similarly unable to achieve 'self-realisation' and therefore an 'anti-class' posture is required to achieve an ecological egalitarianism (Naes 1973: 96-97). It consciously separated class and people and ultimately failed to challenge or even acknowledge capitalism as the cause of environmental degradation. It is capitalism, not the people, that are the guilty parties. Capitalism has brought the planet to the brink. It is not the people that are driven to return increasing profits, or who must out-perform rivals, find bigger markets and newer ways of extracting resources. Capitalism will not be challenged from such an 'ecophilosophy', despite the claim that 'with the decline of socialism, environmentalism becomes the major vantage point of opposition to business-as-usual' (Hay 2002: 341).

To be fair, the development of identity politics was at first criticised by some contemporary Marxists whose primary focus was in political activism. However, few have been able to resist the lure of the 'quick-fix'. Activist politics have developed a conscious focus on the politics of identity, despite having initially decried the ideology. This is true of all political tendencies, be they from Stalinist or ex-Stalinist backgrounds or from the non-Stalinist left. My initial point of reference is Australia, but the cross-over across countries is all but identical. The programmes and policy statements of virtually all political parties with a Marxist orientation (Communist Party of Australia 2016, Socialist Alternative 2007, Socialist Alliance 2015) all declare that they stand for the replacement of capitalism. These political statements are reflected in the majority of parties proclaiming alignment to Marxism around the world. At the same time, these parties strongly advocate for gender, sexual orientation, racial and ethnic policies. While not seeking to diminish such advocacy, the question as to how capitalism is challenged by waging campaigns around what are essentially non-class issues remains unanswered.

Non-class political movements, in the form of identity politics, have built strong constituencies. They have achieved concessions from state institutions, while not eroding state power or capitalism. A problem arises. Identity, as a political focus, limits the potential to present any real challenge to the underlying conditions. Struggles are often arranged around issues of colour, of ethnicity, of religion, of sexuality. Sometimes things become absurd. Gabriel Ignatow, for instance, describes the work of the African-American Environmentalist Association whose goals are 'to increase African-American participation in the environmental movement, promote an African-American point of view in American environmental policy...' (2007: 1).

Some have come to appreciate that people occupy more than one secure identity group. This realisation gave birth to the concept of *intersectionality* in radical political movements. The concept of intersectionality is often attributed to Kimberle Crenshaw. She argues that 'the problem with identity politics is not that it fails to transcend differences...but rather the opposite – that it frequently conflates or ignores intragroup differences' (1993: 1242). She uses the issues of race and gender as a case in point and seeks to broaden the argument to become potentially more inclusive of differences in primary focus. While this theory does take account of the limiting nature of identity politics it remains locked into a non-class approach to understanding inequality. However, regardless of the web of interwoven identities, a problem remains. Marx described the advent of a distribution of labour and the class nature of society, whereby each person 'has a particular, exclusive sphere of activity, which is forced upon him and from which he cannot escape' (Marx and Engels 1964: 44). Marx wrote of the limiting nature of workers being identified by trade or the 'type' of work undertaken. Identification within a much greater group offers a greater capacity to effect change. In this case class identification becomes immensely stronger than that of individual trades. A narrow political alignment based on personal identification, like a designated role in the production process, limits the potential for change.

Political responses to capitalism, globalisation and the alienation that this generates are inescapable. The position of the working class as a force for fundamental change has been relegated, in the thinking of many, to a position of relative insignificance. Prominent 'Marxist' thinking from the 1960s has turned more towards the role that social movement politics can play in the development of a broad anti-capitalist movement. Broad, non-class and supra-class movements have mobilised huge numbers of people and have united diverse sections of the population. For many, social movement politics offers a vehicle to successfully confront capitalism. For others, the very supra-class nature and limitations of programme, inherent in such movements, become clearly defined.

Social movement politics or a bigger identity

Some people do seem to like to go about re-inventing wheels. There is an element of this in social movement politics. The working class exists and cuts across gender, race, ethnicity and sexuality. The working class also exists across continents and is in a constant state of growth. It might seem obvious but such a movement, if organised, is just a little bit greater than any identity group. But no, new wheels or variations on wheels apparently need to be invented. Cue social movement politics.

Identity-based politics are clearly too narrow. Social movement activism consciously seeks to broaden the scope for resistance. While social movement politics have flourished in the period of capitalist globalisation since the 1970s, they have had a long history. Well over a century ago, social movement activism and activists were described as 'a confusion of fussy, fidgety folk, blocking each other and everybody else' (Small 1897: 340). Small's tongue was firmly in his cheek. He was a supporter.

Social movement activism sets itself a huge task. It seeks to build a sense of collective identity that may exceed class identity. Broadly speaking there were 'old' social movements which most usually took the form of trade union activism, while the 'new' forms have tended to move away from any identification with the working class.

Social movement politics have, for many, replaced the working class as a force for change. Plausible arguments are put, describing how 'collective identity replaced class consciousness as the factor that accounts for mobilization and individual attachments to new social movements' (Hunt and Benford 2007: 437). The capacity for social movements to mobilise large numbers is evident. The civil rights movement in the US in the 1960s, the anti-Vietnam, anti-nuclear, environment, the 'Occupy', anti-globalisation and anti-capitalist movements are all testimony to the success that these broad movements have in building a constituency. Sustaining constituencies becomes far more difficult. These movements often share things in common. At face value they might appear to be ideal vehicles to effect change. They are almost exclusively political in character. They make demands upon the state, or more correctly call upon the state for action and they are sincere in their desire to effect social change. The efficacy of these movements becomes an issue that is contested:

In their aim of changing the status quo, social movements face a fundamental dilemma. If they ask for short-term policy changes, they have a greater chance that such changes will occur, but they will not alter, in a fundamental way, existing structures and practices. If instead, movements demand long-term institutional changes, they will encounter more difficulties in realizing such changes...Social movements rarely alter political institutions and only under very restricted conditions (Guigni 1999: xxiv).

Fundamental questions of political theory emerge. They are the questions that Marxists debated a century ago. They are those same nagging questions of reformist or revolutionary paths to change.

Social movement theorists do address both reforming and revolutionary perspectives, but rarely introduce a class dimension to debates. Jeff Goodwin and James Jasper (2009: 4) differentiate between the two forms. They define a 'revolutionary' social movement as one that actively seeks to overthrow the state, while a broader social movement, deemed to be a reforming instrument, 'is a collective, organised, sustained, and non-institutional challenge to authorities, powerholders, or cultural beliefs and practices' (2009: 4). There is a broadly accepted view that the purpose of social movements, and the political agendas they pursue, are primarily aimed at moving society and institutions within that society to a less oppressive position. The echoes to those debates of a century and more ago between Marxist and social-democrat theorists is loud and clear.

The fact that these new social movements have not challenged capitalism in any real sense is a side-issue for some. Self-satisfied claims are made that social movement politics are 'natural self-evident successors of the labour movement' (Olofsson 1988: 16). Gunnar Olofsson argues that the labour movement, as a representation of 'old' class-based politics, is a symbol of social movements whose time has passed. It is a logic that is very much in keeping with the move away from class as a defining point in the social and economic relations of capitalism. Social movements become, inevitably, non-class or supra-class organisations. This is presented as a strength but is ultimately a seriously limiting factor. There is, in all of this, an assumption that there has been a greater degree of success with the new as opposed to the older 'obsolete' movements. It also presupposes a fundamental difference in approach that is not always apparent.

We need to remember that the labour movement activism,

of which the 'new' social movement advocates are so critical, suffered from a process of integration into the capitalist state structure. Ted Wheelwright (1953) traced the trajectory of the trade union movement and of state responses to union activism. He noted three phases in the relationship between the unions and the capitalist state – hostility and attempts at suppression by the state, tolerance but little by way of co-operation, and finally co-operation and partnership with the capitalist state. This incorporation was noted by Trotsky who described the situation in Europe in the 1920s whereby there 'is a powerful international organisation of the trade union bureaucracy. It is thanks to it that the whole structure of capitalism stands upright' (1974: 247-248).

John Macionis (2007) offers an interesting view of newer forms of social movement activism. He highlights four stages that constitute the 'life-cycle' of a social movement. These are success, co-optation, repression or establishment within the mainstream of society. There are striking similarities between his description and that of Wheelwright. That there are clear points of connection between 'old' and 'new' social movements indicate that problems associated with programme and intent remain unresolved. It certainly raises questions as to the perceived purpose of the 'movement'. Eduard Bernstein's (1975: 202) controversial claim that the eventual destination (socialism) is of less importance than the 'movement' is regrettably played out yet again.

Capitalist globalisation and the rise of social movement politics have evolved together. These protests have been both national and international in scope. Some have adopted an 'anti-capitalist' perspective. Others have focussed on war, poverty or environmental issues. Organisers have successfully been able to draw millions of people into protest and political action. The World Social Forum and the 'Occupy' movement, among others, highlighted the discontent that many people were and are feeling. These actions have assumed a growing significance as the globalisation of capitalism has progressed and are a reaction against globalisation. Political responses frequently share a view that economic actions and outcomes can be separated from the globalisation of capitalism – that capitalism and globalisation can be regarded as separate entities. Anti-globalisation becomes, for some, a euphemism for 'deglobalisation'. Confusion becomes the norm. Within this confused state a range of unlikely 'plans' exist. Globalisation might be reversed with the nation-state becoming the vehicle for such a reversal. Social movements might democratise capitalism and make globalisation softer and more caring. Globalisation might be challenged by increasing protectionism. There are a lot of 'might be' scenarios and they have things in common. They are confused, they sow confusion and promote nationalism in the face of capitalist globalisation.

The confusion that theorists surround themselves in is born of the decades of retreat from the essential and core theories of Marxism. The demoralisation and despair that can be seen from so many responses to the crisis that is engulfing the world and capital makes activist practice a shell. It refuses to acknowledge the importance of the single biggest 'social movement' of this or any age – the working class. It can see no way forward and so retreats further into nationalism and nationalist rhetoric. The crimes committed against the working class and against Marxism find voice in populist calls to an amorphous 'anti-capitalism' that can mean anything to anyone. The term anti-capitalist has a range of interpretations and has the potential to confuse and diffuse ideas and arguments. For some, anti-capitalism might mean a struggle for socialism. For others, it might be a movement that looks to a pre-capitalist means of production, or any permutation that lies between these poles. David Harvey (2010), for instance, outlines a range of potential lines along which anti-capitalist movements might run, including anarchist and autonomous movements, traditional labour/socialist political expressions, social movement politics effectively promoting local issues, and identity politics including those of gender, sexuality, ethnicity and race. Ultimately the issue of social movement politics, whether 'old' or 'new', becomes a question of purpose, of motive, of determining what result is either desired or required. This is the point of departure between classical Marxism and those voices who have sought, since the Stalinisation of Marxism, to shift the agenda onto safer ground.

Ultimately it is not so much a case of whether this or that attempt at reforming a movement is the better option. Nor is it a question of how do we make Marxism 'relevant' in the face of a capitalism that remains so obviously in control? It is a question of recognising that there is a crisis, that the crisis stems from a departure from Marxism and that Stalinism and its national programme is anathema to Marxism. It is the recognition of this that allows us to see how those who were either blinded by Stalinism or those in their attempts to by-pass Stalinism, permitted and engaged in a deformation of theory to take place. Until these questions are resolved, capitalism will remain unchallenged.

And still capital remains unchallenged

The shift in Marxist theory, from its focus on the centrality of the working class, to broader, non-class approaches, has seriously limited the potential to oppose capitalist rule. This is shown in a diffused Marxist organisational response to capitalist crisis and, particularly since the 1960s, in social movement theories that fail to offer effective challenge to capitalist rule. The attitude of 'Marxism' to social movement politics has often been ambivalent, although Marxists traditionally sought to provide an understanding of the role of capitalism and class. This has been less evident in recent decades. Richard Flacks makes a stinging observation that 'one of Marx's central analytic strategies…is missing from contemporary theories [of social movements] – namely, his effort to embed power relations in an analysis of the political economy as a whole' (2004: 138). This shift is due to a lack of theoretical clarity that emerged from the crisis in Marxism and from capitalism's ideological ability to obscure and cloud what would otherwise have the potential to invigorate a class-conscious appraisal of issues.

The ability to persuade people that legitimacy rests within a class-based society is enormously enduring. Without going into any protracted analysis of how the state manipulates and 'arranges' the consciousness of people to best suit the ends of the state and of capital, we can reasonably accept the notion outlined by Frances Fox Piven and Richard Cloward of how power is maintained in a class-based state. Power is:

> rooted in the control of coercive force and in control of the means of production. However, in capitalist societies this reality is not legitimated by rendering the powerful divine, but by obscuring their existence...[through] electoral-representative institutions [that] proclaim the franchise, not force and wealth, as the basis for the accumulation of power (1977: 2).

Anyone who would seek to seriously challenge capitalism and to fundamentally alter the economic structures of society must confront this reality. This artificial legitimisation creates the optimum conditions to render movements that seek to oppose capitalism and globalisation powerless. This is despite the often large numbers of people that are drawn into political action.

What remains is an inability to successfully channel discontent. This is particularly the case when anti-capitalist, anti-globalisation movements do not pursue a path to emancipation that seeks to replace capitalism, and this, to be frank, is the reality. When there is talk of developing anything resembling a movement that would seek to challenge capitalism, it remains shrouded in confusion and timidity.

Herein lies a problem for 'Marxism' in the twenty-first century. The role of the working class, once regarded as pivotal to anti-capitalist ideological and organisational movements has, over time, been relegated and diminished. Anti-capitalist and anti-globalist movements have increasingly assumed a non-class and supra-class emphasis. The 'middle class' nature of many of these movements, while briefly mobilising large numbers, has not and cannot develop into a movement that would confront and challenge capitalist rule.

The 1960s saw the rise of a more overtly radicalised middle class. This fuelled the ideological shift by many within the Marxist movement away from the working class. The focus and motivations underlying expressions of middle-class radicalism were highlighted by Frank Parkin (1968) when he drew a distinction between working-class and middle-class radicalism. The middle-class variant was geared less to questions of economic reforms, and more to social reforms which he described as being 'moral' in nature. Parkin's position in the late 1960s closely mirrors that of Marx from the 1840s. Parkin was essentially paraphrasing Marx and Engels' comments regarding 'German or true socialism', that they represented 'not true requirements, but the requirements of Truth; not the interests of the proletariat, but the interests of Human Nature, of Man in general, who belongs to no class, has no reality, who exists in the misty realm of philosophical fantasy' (Marx and Engels 1977: 65-66). This raises important questions. Marxism asserts that the working class is a potentially revolutionary force. How can this claim be justified in the face of a weakening of working-class strength and consciousness?

Marxism has long argued that the working class is a revolutionary class, or at least a class with revolutionary potential. Such attribution separates it from other classes and groups in society. The claim is based primarily on the premise that the source of all wealth, all profit in capitalist relations, is derived from labour, from the surplus value produced by labour. Michael Lebowitz proposes the argument that the working class becomes a 'revolutionary subject' precisely from the struggles that it is forced to undergo:

and, those struggles bring us up against capital. Why? Because capital is the barrier that stands between us and our own development. And it is so because capital has captured the fruits of all civilization, is the owner of all the products of the social brain and the social hand, and it turns our products and the products of workers before us against us—for one sole purpose, which is its own gain, profit. If we are to satisfy our needs, if we are to be able to develop our potential, we must struggle against capital and, in doing so, we working people create ourselves as revolutionary subjects (2012a: 35).

While this is undeniably the case, the growth of middle-class radicalism since the 1960s remains a fact, and a fact that must be taken into consideration. As the crisis in capitalism intensifies, so too does the middle class become threatened. Emmanuel Collado (2010: 1), in describing the 'shrinking' of the middle class, argues that it is financial rather than social or political circumstances that are leading to this threat. Once more we see the Marxian argument of the primacy of the economic at play.

How relevant is Marxism in the age of capitalist crisis? Therborn (2012) speaks of the twentieth century as the century of the working class while the twenty-first century represents a shift to the middle class. It is a construction that is broadly accepted by many theorists and many who would see themselves as 'Marxists'. Therborn accepts that capitalist exploitation and oppression continue and asks who will put their stamp upon the new century and the struggles against capitalism – the 'new' middle class or those he describes as the 'plebeian' masses. Having declared the century of the working class to be over, Therborn ultimately offers a defeatist and demoralised perspective. Marxism cannot simply ignore this or that section of the population, but nor can it be permitted to equivocate. The class nature of society has not changed. The potential and capacity of a globalised working class remains strong. The middle class has increasingly been brought into direct confrontation with capitalism. D'Amato (2006: 100) makes what is possibly an obvious point but one that needs to be stated. The world view of the working class is broadly collectivist while that of the middle class is individualist. These perspectives differ, but they do not preclude a radicalised middle class from playing a significant role, alongside a class-conscious working class. This might appear to be an optimistic assessment given the lack of class consciousness that exists within the working class today and the obvious lack of leadership that entrenches capitalist rule while it remains riven by crisis.

The lack of leadership, a relative lack in class consciousness, the betrayal of theory, are all factors that have permitted capitalism to remain unchallenged, even in the face of increasing crisis. The expansion and acceleration of crisis has compelled capitalism to change. It was, and is, in a constant state of change but the period since the crisis of the 1970s has seen a qualitative change in capitalism. This raises several questions. How and why has this change been manifested? What are the implications for the nation-state and for the working class? How does the ideological edifice of capitalist rule manage to continue to manufacture the fog that still engulfs so many?

Chapter 5

Changes to capitalism and warning bells

It has been well established that Marxism has been seriously undermined, primarily by Stalinism and then by those voices who sought to 'rescue' Marxism from Stalinism. Central elements of Marxist theory have been repudiated and this has led, at least temporarily, to an inability for Marxism to exert any real influence in its struggle to combat and overturn capitalism. Theory has been debunked and practice undermined. If we were to look for winners and losers then the biggest winner in all of this is, undoubtedly, capitalism. The biggest loser has been the working class. While the 'wrecking' ball of Stalinism has splintered and disarmed the working class, capitalism has remained in crisis. Whether it could have survived a united and coherent movement, armed with Marxist theory at the head of a class-conscious working class, is difficult, if not impossible, to say. What can be said, however, is that an accelerated economic crisis has seen capitalism undergo some rather dramatic changes.

These changes have had particular impact on the nation-state as a form of governance and on the working class, as exploitation and inequality grow and insecurity stalks the lives of billions on the planet. While all of this has been going on, there has been an inertia or possibly paralysis on the part of those whose purpose ought to be not only to explain the world but to change it.

Suggesting that there has been a change in capitalism does not imply that the motivation for capitalist development has changed. Its function and 'nature' remain constant. Capitalism is but a stage in the historical evolution of society and economic relations. Consequently, capitalism is in a continual state of motion. Capitalism, in seeking to overcome its inherent and intensifying contradictions, and faced with the threat of economic breakdown, rapidly globalised. The twenty-first century has seen the contradiction between globalised capitalism and national governments become increasingly acute. These developments are all indications of capitalism entering a new stage in its history. This has direct and explosive implications for the working class everywhere.

Capitalism has always tended towards crisis. This has become more visible and more intense as evidenced by the dramatic increase in the power of finance capital (the financialisation of capitalism), the changes in the productive use of capital, and the growing integration of the global economy.

The changes are visible. The idea of anything like a qualitative change in capitalism at first appears to be contradicted by the continued strength of the nation-state and of a return to policies of economic nationalism that are increasingly and dangerously evident in the developed capitalist economies. However, the interaction between an increasingly transnational capitalism and the nation-state structure is the most fundamental contradiction facing capitalism, the working class and indeed Marxism in the twenty-first century. It is all but self-evident that capitalist markets cannot exist without an institutional framework. Capitalist states play two distinct roles – as administrators and innovators. It is as administrator that capitalist states have an on-going and significant role as capitalism seeks to adjust and adapt to the contradictions that impel change.

While the role of the nation-state has been challenged it continues to inhabit a powerful place, both economically and politically and importantly in its capacity to maintain a sense of 'national unity' among the working class. If capitalism has entered a qualitatively new stage, reactions and responses from those most affected will reflect these changes. Capitalist globalisation has intensified social inequality and social discontent. Historically, capitalism has developed against just such a backdrop. The intensification of these phenomena and the response by individual states are further indications of change. Reactions to globalisation and an increased sense of discontent are being increasingly expressed through left- and right-wing populism. States, as 'administrators' and as 'innovators' have sought to contain and channel this discontent.

This, in turn, has serious ramifications for the working class. The rise in nationalist sentiment and the return of economic nationalism reflects the unresolved contradictions between globalisation and the nation-state. There are implicit dangers posed by a resurgence of nationalism, both to capitalism and to the working class. The threat of war hangs in the air as the reality of trade wars leads the world into ever darker corners.

It is all well and good to 'diagnose' changes in capitalism. A range of issues present themselves. Serious thought needs to be given to finding ways to finally resolve the crisis in capitalism. That, of course, must ultimately mean overcoming the cause of the crisis itself. Neither capitalist free trade nor protectionism can resolve the problems facing the working class. What is lacking is a leadership that is independent of the state and the institutions of the state and one that embraces the intrinsic internationalism of the working class. The most pressing contradiction of capitalism is between a globalising economy and a continued reliance on a strong nation-state system. This has manifested itself in a rise in nationalism, with the working class remaining locked into a nationalist perspective. This further limits its capacity to act independently and as a global force to combat capitalism. Generations after the death of Stalin and decades after the collapse of the Soviet Union, the ghost of Stalinism still stalks the world.

The fog machine of capitalist ideology

Capitalism is in a constant state of flux. Some see this as a strength and an ability for renewal due to its alleged resilience. Others point to a weakened capacity for its opposition to, well...

oppose. There have been, since the 1970s, some significant shifts in the way capitalism operates. The rapidity of globalisation and the integration of the economy have huge implications for the working class, and yet, all seems calm and despite growing insecurity, all appears to be in order.

The class nature of society and the crucial role that the state plays in this class-based society is clear. Capitalism and the state enjoy a mutually advantageous relationship. There is also a close connection between class society and the careful use of ideology to foster a semblance of harmony within society. Marx and Engels (1964: 78-79) argued that once the bourgeoisie assumed the ascendancy, it became imperative for the state to preserve the existing balance, by force if necessary. At the same time the link between the bourgeoisie and state is 'more internal and essential than the contingent use of control...the state, as such, is intrinsically a bourgeois form of social relationship' (Sayer 1985: 241).

Capitalist society is framed by class relations and class interests that will always be opposed to one another. To maintain a sense of harmony and accord, the state must therefore limit any obvious manifestations of class antagonism. This task is made easier if the views of the working class can be artificially aligned with those of the ruling class. An effective integration of the working class and of its organisations occurs. This co-option serves to both reduce overt expressions of class antagonism while allowing for an unhindered capitalist development. Over time, and an historically short period of time, this sense of antagonism becomes blurred and is all but erased from the collective memory.

This use of 'ideology' to deliver a required outcome becomes, as Terry Eagleton describes it, a 'process whereby interests of a certain kind become masked, rationalized, naturalized, universalized, legitimized in the name of certain forms of political power' (Eagleton 1991: 202). The careful use of a state ideology legitimises political power and diminishes the capacity for class consciousness. Marx described how the development of capitalism acted to promote such a state of affairs:

> The advance of capitalist production develops a working-class, which by education, tradition, habit, looks upon the conditions of that mode of production as self-evident laws of Nature. The organisation of the capitalist process of production, once fully developed, breaks down all resistance (1986a: 689).

Such has certainly been the case. We need only pause and look around us to see this. Michael Lebowitz (2004: 21-23) makes the point that capitalism maintains its position of ideological power by masking the exploitative nature of the economic system itself. The idea of labour power and the extraction of surplus value, so fundamental to capitalism, are never explicitly divulged. Capitalism, therefore, is not 'visibly' exploitative. This easily leads to a degree of 'mystification' of capital itself. Society, according to Lebowitz's argument, does not appear to depend on capital but rather gives the impression of autonomy. The fact is that workers are not simply dependent on capital, but on particular sections of capital. As these sections are often in competition with each other then so too are individual groups of workers in competition with other workers. This intensifies an already dependent relationship on capital which, in turn, reduces still further the potential for the development of class consciousness.

This situation, whereby class antagonisms are masked, has been labelled false consciousness (Engels 2000) and cultural hegemony (Gramsci 1971: 257-264). Valeriano Ramos Jr describes the essence of Gramsci's perspective:

> In a given hegemonic system, therefore, a hegemonic class

holds state power through its economic supremacy and through its ability to have, among other things, successfully articulated or expressed in a coherent, unified fashion the most essential elements in the ideological discourses of the subordinate classes in civil society (1982).

In other words, state power is maintained by a combination of economic power and control of the broad machinery of state: the institutions of control. Credit must be given for a job well done. The effectiveness of state control and of its ability to evoke a feeling, not merely of acceptance, but of willing acceptance on the part of the working class, has been extraordinarily successful.

This success has been enhanced through carefully and consciously integrating the organisations of the working class into the organisations of the state. This integration has long been a reality. Trade unions became legitimate and, in a similar way, political expressions of working-class ideology became an accepted and acceptable component in the life of the capitalist state. Social-democratic parties became legitimised within the capitalist nation-state; legitimised, increasingly integrated into that state structure and actively promoting the values and mores of the state, even if this meant acting against the interests of the class they were formed to represent. Stalinist political expression in the West was in reality no less integrated into state structures, and especially when considered in the context of 'communist' leadership of trade unions in so many countries that led more often to harmony than to challenge.

A consequence of this integration has been a shrinking of working-class independence. This state of affairs – the inability of the 'legitimate' organisations of the working class to act independently – is by no means a recent development in state and class relations. 'Capitalism is less and less willing to reconcile itself to the independence of trade unions. It demands of the reformist bureaucracy...that they become transformed into its political police before the eyes of the working class' (Trotsky 1972: 11). Such a formulation accords with the observations of Michael Mann where he argues, decades later, that 'to the extent that trade unions pursue economic and job control issues separately and the latter defensively, and to the extent that they do not pursue wider issues of work control, they operate to weaken workers' class consciousness' (1973: 25). Recent decades have seen less and less actions, even defensive ones, on the part of the unions. The unions have, in fact, acted against the best interests of their own members.

The capitalist state has managed, through careful and calculated use of the ideological armoury at its disposal, to maintain a semblance of harmony and class unity. It has been necessary for the stability of what is, after all, an inherently unstable mechanism to function. Such a situation poses enormous difficulties for those seeking an independent movement for emancipation. Murray Smith (2014: 322-323) describes the crisis of leadership that exists and how the degree of working-class consciousness that does exist remains entrenched within a framework of reformist and state-sponsored mechanisms. At the same time the contradictions that plague capitalist development remain unresolved and that final and most crucial contradiction remains the contradiction between a globalising capitalism and the nation-state.

Capitalist globalisation: why the rush?

Despite all that has happened in the past century and in the face of what is happening, the hands of Marx's 'grave-diggers' remain firmly tied. Before the knots can be undone, it is necessary to look at capitalism and to the twists and turns it makes to survive. The driving force behind capitalism is its need to expand. To do otherwise is to court disaster. To recognise this is to recognise the impossibility of clinging to anything resembling a nationalist 'way forward'. Marx and Engels noted that, 'the bourgeoisie has through its exploitation of the world market given a cosmopolitan character to production and consumption in every country. To the great chagrin of Reactionists, it has drawn from under the feet of industry the national ground on which it stood' (1977: 39). Trotsky described the growing tendency towards globalisation in terms of 'the future development of world economy...a ceaseless struggle for new and ever new fields of capitalist exploitation' (1973: 22-23).

Marx (1974: 539) also explained how capital must not only eliminate spatial boundaries in order to develop a world market, but that it also must seek to reduce time as a factor in this development, thereby promoting the most expansive market possible. The underlying motivation for this development of capitalism to become an increasingly global phenomenon is the expansion of capital accumulation, the quest for profit and the ever-growing need to at least maintain the level of profit. The dynamism of such economic development across the globe has both positive and negative implications, at once polarising wealth and poverty, while still allowing for capital accumulation and the development of abundance (Dunn 2009: 158).

A key factor in the drive to globalisation lies in a central argument of Marx; described as the law of the falling rate of profit (*Capital Vol. 3* 1986b: 211-231). Among a range of options that capital can employ to remove such an obstacle, or at least to postpone and forestall the worst outcomes, is to continually expand and to internationalise its relations. This means, in effect, a continual motion and an endless battle to survive. The similarity between this and the necessity of a shark to keep swimming or drown is always an interesting one. This inherent contradiction between the need to expand and the tendency for falling rates of profit has been and remains central to globalisation. The 'golden age' of capitalism in the period from the end of World War II and the crisis of the 1970s, coinciding with the abandonment, by so many, of Marxist theory, saw this element of Marxism ignored or denied. The globalisation from the 1970s, however, is a direct response to this tendency for profits to fall.

Two related propositions of Marx, relating to the development of capitalist globalisation, are worthy of note. The first is that merchant capital is inherently destructive to colonial economies while industrial capital constructs new economies (Marx 1969b: 107). The second, that capitalism as an inevitably expansionary process, must destroy older, pre-existing economic systems in order to create new ones (Marx 1975: 200-201). These arguments eloquently describe the effects of colonialism and imperialism in the nineteenth and early twentieth centuries. Imperialism, in Marxist thought, was regarded as the 'penetration and spread of the capitalist system into non-capitalist or primitive capitalist areas of the world' (Warren 1980: 3).

Nothing much changes in this regard. Beverley Silver (2006: 3-23) describes the contemporary situation whereby global capital flows serve to actively build new industrial working-class movements, as capitalism constructs new industrial bases across the world. Understanding the processes of capitalist globalisation and the motivations for such a rapid rate of development in recent decades is intimately connected to Marx's description of the unfolding of global capitalism.

Capital flows are elements of a constant drive to maintain a high degree of profitability. The period since the economic crisis years of the 1970s is portrayed as a period marked by stagnating profits, and a general decrease in wages across states. We must remember that the very *raison d'etre* of capitalism as an economic formation is to expand.

The rapidity of capitalist globalisation from the 1970s was accompanied by a dramatic shift in manufacturing away from industrialised countries and to the developing world. Capitalism sought to minimise the harm coming from the growing crisis; the rapid economic downturn and a reduction in profit levels. As an indicator of capitalist integration, and as a reaction to the crisis, production was increasingly transferred overseas. This certainly assisted profitability but also had the obvious effect of producing mass unemployment along with a general reduction in wages. The 'great contradiction of the age' was becoming clearer and uglier. Hans-Peter Martin and Harald Schumann (1997: 7) show how wages in the industrial world have tended to fall. Capitalism, in its quest to maintain its growth-centred sense of equilibrium, inevitably creates 'winners' and 'losers'. This becomes apparent both in individual nation-states and when outcomes between states are considered.

As globalisation of the economic and political structures has quickened, so too has the role of global institutions been held up to scrutiny. The neoliberal economic agenda has been facilitated, in the estimation of many writers, by the increased power of the International Monetary Fund, the World Bank and significantly with the inception of the WTO. Michel Chossudovsky (1998: 35) regards the WTO's role as effectively supervising national trade policies in the interests of the transnational corporations. An even more strident accusation is that the WTO is 'the archetypal transnational institution of the new epoch' (Robinson 2004: 117). In somewhat softer tones is the appraisal that multinational corporations and states work in tandem to promote common objectives (Nash 2000: 264).

The continuing globalisation of capital and the political ramifications that this represents have long been features of capitalist relations. The theoretical 'fog' that engulfed contemporary Marxism has, to its shame, done little to arm those who have most to lose. Globalisation did not simply fall from the sky but is an on-going and inevitable process of capitalist development. The changes in capitalist relations that are evident are revolutionary in character. It is in the financialisation of capital that changes in capitalism are best observed. The continuing separation of capitalism from the restrictions of state structures is but one indication that things are changing in capitalist relations. These relational changes are inescapable for capitalism as it seeks to overcome the inherent contradictions and tendency towards crisis.

So, what about the nation-state?

Capitalism has long sought to overcome its contradictions, but without success. The contradictions that have driven globalisation have not been eliminated, but on the contrary, the most acute of capitalism's contradictions, between increasingly globalised economic structures and political formations based on national governments, just continue to sharpen.

Capitalism has long since broken the bounds of the nation-state. This has been a fact of economic and political life for a very long time (Trotsky 1996). Productive capital no longer resides within the confines of individual nation-states. At the same time, the nation-state, as an organisational structure, is a reality and, largely due to that same ideological fog machine, a reality that claims the emotional support of the great majority of the world's population.

Capitalism requires stable governance. This has been magnificently delivered by the state. Simultaneously, capitalism, as a globalising entity, must break any restrictive fetters. This problem is compounded by the constant drive to counter and forestall the tendency for the rate of profit to fall. It is in this context that a new stage of capitalism can be observed. The growing influence of finance capital in the face of the crisis of capitalism that erupted in the 1970s sped up the development of a new global working class while destroying industrialisation in the developed economies. The contradictory relationship between individual state structures and an increasingly borderless economic system has prompted some to question the long-term viability of the nation-state and others to question globalisation itself.

It is hardly surprising, therefore, that the intensification of capitalist globalisation has prompted discussion as to the future and viability of the nation-state. There are those who argue that 'markets' are now more powerful than states. This has led to claims (Ohmae 1995) that the nation-state has no real role in the global economy. Still others, such as UK economist Ann Pettifor (2008), call for the threatened state to be 'upsized' as a way of maintaining, or rather reclaiming, a lost autonomy that has come from a globalised economic system. There is an obvious paradox in all of this. The state must simultaneously facilitate the development of an increasingly borderless capitalism while safeguarding political realities within national borders. And so, after watching this dangerous juggling act, the nation-state is declared, by some, to be obsolete, while others call for its strengthening. The muddlers of theory have unfortunately led many into a muddlesome sort of world. The theory that drives classical Marxism is, however, not a muddled one.

Marxism maintains that a primary purpose of the state is to facilitate capitalist development. While the role of the state has not fundamentally altered, capitalism's development has necessarily placed a strain on that relationship. This has always been the case but has become more acute as capitalism has transformed itself into a truly globalised entity. Marx's view of the nation-state and of its future was clear. He maintained that the development and expansion of capitalism would ultimately weaken any semblance of independence for the state.

The state's dual role of facilitating capitalism's development while maintaining peace and harmony at home bumps into a number of interconnected problems. The crisis of capitalism has prompted changes in capitalist relations (financialisation, changes in the productive use of capital, and an increased integration of capitalism). This has led to an intensification of inequality and social disharmony which in turn has manifested itself in a broad, anti-capitalist, anti-globalisation sentiment. There has been a reaction against austerity, growing poverty and a general tendency towards social and economic insecurity. Populist movements have grown. A perceptible rise in nationalist sentiment is the result. The state has carefully fostered this sentiment, with the result that the working class has remained locked into a nationalist framework, with leaderships that maintain a national perspective. This has been made easier by the complicity that comes with workers organisations being integrated into the state. Stalinism's legacy and the debt that capitalism owes to Stalinism is once more on display.

The concept of a national state, in conjunction with national governance and national economic organisation, is an entrenched one. This is despite the fact that it is a construction framed by and in an historical period of time. This needs to be kept in the forefront of debates concerning globalisation and the state. Ellen Wood, for example, found 'it hard to foresee the day when capital will stop being organized on national principles' (2002: 29). The point is, however, that neither the nation-state, nor capitalism for that matter, are immutable but exist in an historical context. What also needs to be borne in mind is that the nation-state is ultimately a political formation and not a geographical location.

The era of state-based autonomous economies has passed. Capitalism has become increasingly integrated. Susan Strange (1997a) famously wrote of the retreat of the state and the decline of state authority in the face of globalisation. She argued that where 'states were once the masters of markets, now it is the markets which, on many critical issues, are the masters over the governments of states' (1997a: 4). Strange contended that while individual firms might be described as 'American' or 'British', this ought not to obscure the fact of global integration and that dramatic changes in financial structures clearly indicate changes in capitalist production relations (Strange 1997b).

Lathi Jotia (2011) is among a number of writers who have sought to explain the political and economic realities facing the nation-state. He argues that the nation-state operates largely to arrange domestic issues as a means of facilitating the overarching needs of global capitalism and that it has come to the point where 'global change dictates terms under which the national governments should function' (Jotia 2011: 246). The potential dislocation for states is further highlighted by Vito Tanzi who points out that 'globalization is forcing countries to abide more and more...by the rules of the market. Countries that ignore these rules are now likely to pay a much greater price than they did when economies were closer...national governments are likely to see their economic role reduced' (1998: 13).

The fact that globalisation is affecting the nation-state is obvious. What is less certain is the intensity of this effect. As with most things, the theorists scramble for answers and react to events. Paths quickly diverge. William Robinson, for instance, looks to a future that he believes to be close at hand, whereby the nation-state and its role is superseded by a transnational capitalist class (1998: 567). Others, not wanting to 'frighten the horses', make the claim that there is nothing particularly special about capitalist globalisation (Hirst and Thompson 1999). While they might tell us that 'there is nothing to see here', the fact remains that there is quite a bit to see in what has been and remains an on-going globalisation of production. This means an increase in international and global economic activity, and that can only lead to greater levels of economic integration. This inevitably has implications for the nation-state. Paul Hirst and Graheme Thompson actively seek to downplay the significance of the globalisation of capitalism. They clearly wish to expose what they claim to be the 'myth' of globalisation in order to persuade 'reformers of the left and conservatives who care for the fabric of their societies that we are not helpless before uncontrollable global processes' (1999: 7). While the contending arguments of the hyperglobalists and sceptics can make interesting reading, they do not offer anything like a satisfactory response to questions of how to combat capitalism itself. Robinson's (2004) view that there needs to be a movement towards a 'global democratisation' remains vague and ill-defined. Similarly, to dismiss globalisation as a 'myth', limits working-class response to capitalism to nationally-based reactions to what are increasingly globalised issues.

What remains is crisis. It is a crisis that has serious ramifications for a working class that is at once increasingly globalised but still confined by nationalist sentiments and symbols. The debates as to the health of the nation-state in the face of globalised capitalism must, therefore, take into account questions of nationalism as an ideological response. Nationalism, in the eyes of the theorists, can be either good, bad or quite possibly ugly. Craig Calhoun (1997) sees nationalism as a positive and even progressive thing, which given its track record is difficult to accept. Ronaldo Munck promotes the view that 'nationalism continues to articulate social discontent and is the source of new solidarities' (2010: 51). If by solidarity he means something like the coming together of far-right leader Nigel Farage, former Trotskyist Claire Fox and former left-wing Labour Party member George Galloway in the Brexit Party, then it is an idea whose time ought not to have come. Michael Hardt and Antonio Negri offer a contrasting perspective. They argue that capitalist globalisation, or in their terminology, 'empire', is unstoppable and 'a step forward in order to do away with any nostalgia for the power structures that preceded it' (2000: 43). Their warm embrace recognises that capitalism is undoubtedly a globalising force, and is compelled to be such a force, but needs to be reminded that capitalism is still firmly connected with individual nation-states. This is seen first and foremost in the political role that the state plays and in the class relations that are evident. Class, after all, matters. The working class has grown dramatically in global terms as capitalism has developed new centres of production. Nationalism has been used to ensure that there are no dangerous outbreaks of unity within the global working class. Workers are encouraged to find common cause with their own bourgeoisies and are pitted against each other. In this sense there is very little to separate early twentieth century expressions of nationalism from early twenty-first century nationalist sentiments.

The nation-state, as a political institution, will either strengthen or adapt to globalisation and the qualitative changes in capitalism. State structures will, however, be shaped both by external influences stemming from the requirements of globalised capital and from internal factors as individual states respond to the pressures linked to globalisation (Cox 1987: 253). The effects of globalisation are being felt across all societies and states. We see a world of stagnating and falling profits, a tendency towards decreasing wages share and social and political fragmentation affecting developed and developing states alike. Inequality has risen sharply. Social cohesion has weakened. This is less a result of political and economic policy and more a result of changes in capitalist relations that have been determined by the growing crisis in capitalism. As always, the working class will be most affected.

The crisis and the working class

Despite all that separates the variants of 'contemporary' Marxism from classical Marxist theory, there are some areas that nobody can dispute. All contending schools of thought recognise that inequality and social disharmony are growing. There is a generally held consensus that things are changing, but then consensus quickly starts to unravel. This is hardly surprising. There is a close connection between the shifts that capitalism has made and the dramatic rise in inequality, and the inevitable social discontent that accompanies inequality. Those most affected, the working class, remain powerless in their quest for emancipation. They remain caught in entanglements of nationalist rhetoric and a retreat into national responses to global crises. Where the mirage of unity between 'Marxists' evaporates, is around the differing attitudes to theory and practice in relation to the working class and to the role that the working class has in challenging capitalism.

Inequality and discontent are connected, and their growth has been linked to the rapidity of capitalist globalisation. The rise in social discontent has been seen in both anti-globalisation movements and, more recently, in a decided upsurge of working-class unrest. This is also evident in the growth, in developed economies, of both left- and right-wing political and nationalist movements. The global integration of capitalist relations has particularly affected the working class. Unemployment remains high, industrial and manufacturing production continues to flow from the industrialised states, and welfare state structures continue to be eroded, almost to the point of extinction. Ultimately, this crisis is a consequence of capitalist globalisation. The implications are obvious.

It is almost pointless, almost meaningless to speak of the growing concentration of wealth into fewer hands. No sooner are statistics produced than they become obsolete. In 2002, many were horrified to read that just three of the wealthiest families in the world enjoy an income equivalent to the poorest 600 million. In 2002, Jan Piertese reported on the growth of social inequality since the Industrial Revolution. In 1820, the gap between the richest and poorest 20 per cent of the world's population was 3:1. In 1997 it had moved to a ratio of 74:1 (Piertese 2002: 11025). Then things got worse and got worse rapidly. Oxfam figures show that the world's richest 62 individuals control the same wealth as the poorest 3.5 billion people (Oxfam 2016). Credit Suisse (2015) research reveals that nearly three-quarters of the world's population have a per-capita wealth of less than $10,000. The richest 8 per cent of the population own 84.6 per cent of global wealth. Pieterse asks, 'what kind of world economy grows and yet sees poverty and global inequality rising steeply?'

(2002:1036). The answer to his question is not simply capitalism, but a qualitatively changed capitalism that exists in conditions of irresolvable crisis.

International institutions, analysts and activists all acknowledge that a fundamentally new stage of crisis has emerged. A report issued by the IMF (2015) states that:

> Widening income inequality is the defining challenge of our time. In advanced economies, the gap between the rich and poor is at its highest level in decades. Inequality trends have been more mixed in emerging markets and developing countries (EMDCs), with some countries experiencing declining inequality, but pervasive inequities in access to education, health care, and finance remain (Dabla *et al* 2015: 4).

Inequality in OECD countries is at its highest since records began. The rise in inequality has been reflected in a growth of part-time and casualised labour. Joint ILO/OECD (2015) research has shown that for decades, labour's share of income has lost ground to capital.

ILO (2015) statistics show that in 2015 as many as 75 per cent of all workers across the globe fell into the informal category – either as temporary or short-term employees. The growth of capitalist globalisation is mirrored in the growth of the global working class. It is estimated that the global workforce will have reached 3.5 billion by 2030. One factor that the working class in the OECD and in the developing world have in common is a growing sense of insecurity. The dilemma that faces the nation-state, as both administrator of capitalism and simultaneously as competitor against other states and against a transnational capital, is clear. The dilemma for the working class within these nation-states is not always so clearly stated.

Capitalism and inequality are inextricably linked. While this is an obvious fact, so many 'Marxists' still choose to disregard the working class, who are the first to suffer and who, we might remind these theorists, produce the wealth that is then taken from them. Marx (1986d) was in no doubt that inequality is a necessary component of the wages system. It is an argument that goes to the very core of the relationship between capital and labour. Capitalism uses physical and intellectual labour as a commodity. Marx then went on to declare 'the cry for an *equality of wages* rests, therefore, upon a mistake, an *insane* wish never to be fulfilled...to clamour for *equal or even equitable retribution* on the basis of the wages system is the same as to clamour for *freedom* on the basis of the slavery system' (1986d: 208-209 emphasis in the original).

The changes in capitalism that have been evident in recent decades, as it strives to maintain profitability, have affected how states operate. Globalised markets have provided the motivation and impetus for investors to move capital from traditionally regulated economic centres to the less regulated. This initially resulted in accelerated global economic growth but has resulted in increasing instability and insecurity for the working class. What is particularly significant is that the rate of economic growth appears to have stagnated or at least is growing at an unacceptably slow rate (IMF 2016). While this reflects the underlying problems in capitalism as a crisis-prone system, the fact remains that globalisation was, and is, an attempt to rapidly accelerate economic growth to forestall and circumvent crises stemming from falling profit rates, but is, at the very best, a temporary fix.

Social disharmony and discord are evident but effective challenges have not materialised. There are a range of reasons why this is so, and all remain centred around some key issues. The working class remains firmly attached to the physical and psychological boundaries of the nation-state. The state plays a fundamental role in achieving this. Stalinism and those latter-day 'Marxist' theorists have done a great service to the state in ensuring that the working class remain wedded to the concepts of nationalism and nationalist symbolism. While Marxism traditionally stressed that the working class, if it was to gain emancipation from capitalism, must accept its internationalism (Marx and Engels 1977: 74), the strength of nationalism and nationalist sentiment has remained. It is clear that nationalism and nationalist sentiment has been growing. Nationalism has been carefully nurtured and remains entrenched in the thinking of the working class and in the minds of many whose stated perspective is the struggle against capitalism.

There is an absurdity in all of this, but the future cannot be one that allows for such absurdity. Theorists from the Marxist tradition all too frequently appear happy to remain locked into a national response to what is ultimately a global question. Capitalism occupies an international terrain. To wage what ends up being a localised struggle sets dangerous limitations. This has become the default position, but it need not be so. Working-class discontent has traditionally been expressed through trade union activities which become acutely limited by nationally-based responses to global problems. If we take such propositions to their absurd conclusion, we see Charlotte Yates (2003: 239) arguing that the Canadian Auto Workers Union successfully built an identity around class and radical nationalism. Such a proposition, that 'identity' can be developed by a unity of class and nationalism, is dubious at best. The issues that occupied European Marxism in the period immediately preceding World War I clearly defined two separate responses. Marxists called for a class-based, and therefore internationalist, response but nationalism and an identification with national bourgeoisies remained the dominant perspective. Working-class discontent, in the past decade, has shifted, with less emphasis on overt anti-globalisation, anti-capitalist rhetoric to more pronounced nationalist expressions of dissent. Such responses indicate a serious lack of an effective leadership and the presence of the nationalist perspectives that still dominate the thinking of many and which are engendered and promoted by the state.

There is also a tendency among activists and scholars to offer what appear to be radical propositions but then to ultimately vacillate. This is, to some extent, an understandable tendency. The sorry history of Stalinism has so besmirched the concept of resolute struggle against capitalism and, therefore, for revolutionary change. The future becomes uncertain. Challenge becomes a fearful thing. It is easy to become demoralised and defeatist, even without acknowledging it. Robinson (2004: 178), for instance, after building a theory to 'explain' the rise of a transnational ruling class and the end of the nation-state as an organisational unit, concludes his arguments by calling for a broad 'democratisation' of global society. Edward Webster, Rob Lambert and Andries Bezuidenhout (2008) are prepared to go so far as to see a 'necessity' to engage in utopian thinking. The central contradictions of capitalism, however, remain. What also remains is the result of decades of internecine struggle within Marxism that have resulted in the very lack of leadership that allows capitalism to survive and inequality to grow.

Finding a way out of the labyrinth

Stalinism, and those 'rescuers of Marxism', have, unwittingly, assisted capitalism to withstand existential crisis. Capitalism remains defined by crisis and, while inequality and social discontent have grown, no tangible threat to capitalism has emerged. The contradictions that at once threaten to tear capitalism apart have also served to drive it towards globalisation. These include the private nature of production and the social nature of the process of production, the drive to maximise profit in the face of a tendency for profit rates to fall, and what is of particular significance, the drive to globalised capitalist relations while maintaining and relying on the nation-state as a political mechanism. Marxist polemic revolves around capitalism's ability, or lack of ability, to resolve potential crisis. None of these issues have been resolved and nor can they while capitalism remains. On the contrary, they have become more acute. The changes that are observable in capitalism – the financialisation of capital, the change in the use of productive capital, the integration of capitalism into a global market – have all failed to resolve these contradictions. Capitalism's relationship with the nation-state is its most acute and irresolvable contradiction.

This contradiction, between the globalisation of capitalism and the continued importance and strength of the nation-state, assumes special significance when considered alongside the structural changes that have occurred in capitalism. The nation-state, as administrator of capitalism, has been required to 'manage' a reality marked by intensification of both inequality and social discontent. Nationalist symbols and sentiment have been promoted with the view of building a sense of national unity in the face of growing economic and political difficulties and dislocations. Such an exercise, as history has shown, and the body count from wars of and around nationalism attests, is not without danger.

Debates, in the most recent past, have focussed on the 'return' to economic nationalism. Economic nationalism is, of course, the very antithesis of capitalist globalisation and yet it is growing in direct proportion to capitalism's changes and its globalisation. Sam Pryke defines economic nationalism as 'the attempt to create, bolster and protect national economies in the context of world markets' (2012: 290). The promotion of protectionist measures within national economies in the last few years has been obvious. While fingers have been pointed at Trump as being somehow personally responsible for this, it remains that he is simply a representation of the crisis that is affecting global capitalism and the nation-state structures. If *the* Trump did not exist, then *a* Trump would be found. The WTO points to a 'relapse in G20 economies' efforts at containing protectionist pressures. Not only is the stockpile of trade-restrictive measures continuing to increase, but also more new trade restrictions were recorded' (WTO 2016: 4). Since then, trade wars have become the norm. A decade earlier, former Chairman of the US Federal Reserve Ben Bernanke had cautioned against such an economic shift and the negative consequences it might have for the global economy.

All of this has an eerie similarity to conditions that existed a century ago. Martin Wolf (2004: 37) describes the attempt by capitalist states to reverse the trend towards globalisation that occurred at the end of the nineteenth century. He points out that economic nationalism led to militarism and imperialism. Free trade was stifled, and war was the ultimate and inevitable result. The motivations behind national states to enter into such a contradictory position is both a response to economic downturn and an attempt to ease the fears and concerns of domestic populations that are increasingly facing difficult economic outcomes. The simplistic nationalist rhetoric becomes ever more shrill.

Nationalism, that most resilient of phenomena, has been carefully and consciously engendered by capitalism. The use of emotive symbolism and the ethos of nationalism is a deliberate act of social control in order to manipulate consciousness. Eric Hobsbawm noted that it is 'highly relevant to that comparatively recent historical innovation, the "nation", with its associated phenomena: nationalism, the nation-state, national symbols, histories and the rest. All these rest on exercises in social engineering' (2004: 13).

Nationalism and, in this context, economic nationalism, pits one nation against another and by implication one worker against another There are implicit dangers for national economies and for the working class in such a perspective. Using the case of the post-Soviet period in Russia, David Szakonyi (2007) describes the potential, in the exercising of economic nationalism, to create both internal and external 'enemies' as a means of building a narrow national unity.

The working class, under protectionist conditions, is encouraged to view the working class of 'competing' nations as rivals for jobs. The migrant is accused of stealing jobs. The job-thieves, of course, are those who move production from state to state in search of sustainable and increased profits. These calls are often combined with appeals to freedom and the danger of a loss of freedom. Marx (1956: 251) warned against the abstract use of the term 'freedom', reminding people that such a term, in a class society, ultimately refers to the freedom that capital enjoys in maintaining its position of dominance. The promotion of nationalist perspectives echoes political and economic debates dating back a century when free trade and protectionist debates flourished in the lead up to World War I. What is fundamentally different in this twenty-first century version of the debate is that protectionism and economic nationalism are even less viable options.

While protectionism offers little prospect for benefit to the working class, the call to free trade has similarly provided few benefits and has promoted inequality. 'Marxists' have often struggled with these alternative paths. Marx once declared that he was a supporter of free trade because it hastened the social revolution. He also argued that free trade was simply the freedom of capital. 'It does not matter how favourable the conditions under which the exchange of commodities takes place, there will always be a class which will exploit and a class which will be exploited' (Marx 1956: 250). Marxist theory cannot equivocate, and nor can it privilege one capitalist economic theory, or policy, over another.

While this is so, a state of confusion as to how best to promote challenge becomes so very obvious. As with the Seattle protests, there was a sense of unanimity in response to, and protest at, the failed *Multilateral Agreement on Investment* in the late 1990s. On one hand the 'left' seeks to combat globalisation by promoting nationalism and on the other hand recognises and cautions against the dangers of nationalism. Andrew Gamble (2009: 149-150) argues that the 'left' had traditionally encompassed protectionism in its various programmes and that in recent years both right and left have employed protectionist rhetoric. Unfortunately, his analysis is correct. It supports the premise that the consciousness of the working class has been manipulated by the state. It explains how nationalism has been so easily employed by the state, and especially in limiting any sense of class consciousness. Nationalism is a political tactic that has been used to maintain a sense of unity. It is an expression of economic response to crisis and has seriously weakened the capacity for independent organisation of the working class. In the meantime, capitalism remains unchallenged.

While economic nationalism is resurgent, the capitalist economy remains globalised and increasingly integrated. Anup Shah (2011) shows that 1318 transnational corporations account for 60 per cent of global wealth with the most powerful 147 of these corporations controlling 40 per cent of the total global output and wealth. Fifty-one per cent of the biggest 'economies' in the world are individual corporations and 41 per cent of these are based in the US. The European Commission (2016) indicates that multinational corporations now control more than half of all international trade. The promotion of nationalism, politically and economically, as a means of 'opposing' globalisation is a dangerous idea, creates impossible dreams and will not end well for those most affected by the continued existence of capitalism.

The contradiction between globalised capitalism and a renewed sense of nationalism is disturbingly apparent in the drift, by major economic powers, towards trade blocs and confrontation between 'competitors'. The proposed construction of the Trans-Pacific Partnership was a case in point. The bloc, while professing to 'unite' numbers of regional economies, would only have served to exacerbate tensions between China and the US. There are fears that, as the crisis of capitalism intensifies, the threat to global stability will also intensify. Peter Holmes, in the *NATO Review*, repeats what he calls an 'adage' that 'if goods don't cross frontiers, soldiers will' (2009). He sees a real possibility of a return to the conditions that dominated thinking in the 1930s. Global trade has fallen, and he fears a return to protectionist policies. Since he wrote those uncomfortable words, things have deteriorated alarmingly. He lists a variety of 'threats' with China and Russia being prominent on his list. What remains the most critical of contradictions facing capitalism remains unresolved and is unable to be resolved. This is so because it is a contradiction of capitalism and while capitalism remains then so too will the contradictions that plague it.

Herein lies a dilemma for Marxism and for the working class. We have witnessed capitalism undergoing significant changes for decades. It still requires a strong nation-state as political administrator. Nation-states and residual national capitalism must vie with one another for dominance. While this has been playing out, the working class, as the victim of capitalist exploitation, has been forced to wander in a labyrinth that has its roots in Stalinism and in responses to Stalinism. Leadership must develop that will have the capacity to combat and effectively confront capitalism. It remains the only realistic means of resolving the contradictions of globalised capitalism and the nation-state. It remains the only way out of the labyrinth.

Chapter 6

The promise of Marxism

Opinion polls in the US have been sending worrying messages to capital. Fifty-seven per cent of the American population are now saying that socialism is not such a bad idea after all. Similar figures are appearing in Australian polls and around the world. It is not difficult to understand why this is happening. Capitalism simply does not deliver, and people are seeing this in all its stark reality. There is after all nothing very positive to say about an economic and political system that drives people into poverty and despair, that alienates, commodifies and treats people so poorly and threatens the planet with war and environmental destruction. But if socialism is being seen as something better, why is this not being reflected in a mass political movement for socialism? Sadly, the stain of Stalinism still lingers. Dan Taylor, unwittingly, shows how this works in practice:

> Just as there is no positive capitalism, making an old argument for something seemingly opposite like communism is also pretty suspect. Such an idealistic system is very difficult to establish in practice without resorting to totalitarian measures to ensure its own security from war by external capitalist states (2013: 9).

Herein lies the rub! A lot of people seem to know what they don't want, they know what is bad for them, but are uneasy or unwilling to be seen to align themselves to something that deservedly has such a bad reputation. I am not speaking of socialism, or of communism, and definitely not Marxism in this context. The bad reputation belongs to Stalinism. The fact that Marxism and the mutation that is Stalinism have nothing in common has been forgotten. The path to challenge becomes blurred. Political expressions of Marxism become equally besmirched by Stalinist practices. Marxist, or communist, or revolutionary political parties are looked at as being highways to totalitarianism, to planned austerity, to a loss of freedom. Moving beyond such bleak scenarios is no easy task but is a necessary one.

If we are serious about addressing the need to not merely explain but to change the world, then it is important to fully recognise the significance of analyses that disregard, diminish and withdraw from the very things that make Marxism what it is. We need to refocus, briefly, on whether Marxism can address the problems posed by twenty-first century capitalism. Marxist responses to capitalism must reflect the changes that are apparent, but the additional problem of multiple 'Marxisms' must, once and for all, be resolved. This problem is reflected in the decades-long debates of 'reform or revolution', as well as the role of the working class, and the fundamental issues that stem from the Stalinisation of theory and practice.

This, in turn, forces us to look again at the crisis in Marxism and whether a resolution is possible, or even desirable. This becomes a defining question for Marxism, its purpose, its role, both now and into the future. While polemic and debate naturally allow for theory and ideas to grow, it has come at the cost of the 'practice' of Marxism. Marxism's purpose is irrevocably tied to the success or failure of the development of a political movement of the working class. The most significant and fundamental question is what form of political expression this will be. For Marxists, class matters. This is never more obvious than when the issue of the working class as a 'revolutionary subject' is addressed. While there is a consensus, of sorts, among the varieties of 'Marxism' that a new society is required and that the world needs to change, there remains a reticence among many within contemporary Marxism about how change might be effected. This is understandably connected to a sense of fear of failure that exists in the 'shadow' of Stalinism. Questions of spontaneity and leadership also inevitably surface, as does the potential to harness the spontaneous events of protest into more overt class-conscious activity.

What, then, is Marxism's purpose and future, if not to seek to challenge capitalism and replace it with a saner, more rational world? Marxism has proven to be a valuable analytical tool and has the capacity to trace the trajectory of capitalism. This, however, is not and can never be enough. Marxism's ultimate purpose is to combat and challenge capitalism, with a view to fundamentally changing the world. How can this be achieved? This is the biggest question that faces us all. It is a pointless exercise to point the finger at what is wrong with the world and to 'hope' for something better. What is needed is to find a way forward. The theory of Marxism is certainly the right vehicle. How that theory is presented, how practice can be formulated, how mobilisation can be achieved, are all questions, not for the future but for the immediate here and now. Finding answers to these questions will finally prove Marxism's credentials.

Marxism and twenty-first century capitalism

There are some essential truths that need to be re-stated, even if briefly. Marxism has historically sought to respond to changes in capitalism. This has led to disputation and dislocation within Marxist theory and practice. Marxist theorists have shown an enduring capacity to analyse developments within capitalism, but this has often been at the expense of what remains the core function of Marxism; an organisational and leadership role that can effectively challenge capitalism. While being intensely critical of much that passes for contemporary Marxist theory, it must be acknowledged that from the Stalinisation of the Russian Revolution and the limitations this imposed on the development of Marxist thought, to the subsequent crisis in Marxism, there has been an on-going movement to develop a Marxist ideology that would remain relevant. Unfortunately, serious errors have been made that have damaged Marxist theory and therefore practice. The result has been an unnecessary question mark that has hung for too long over Marxism's capacity to respond and to finally resolve the final contradictions of capitalism and in so doing overcome and replace capitalism with a saner, more rational political and economic system that serves the best interests of all.

There is a crisis in capitalism that threatens the world. In responding to that crisis, it is well to seriously re-appraise Marxist theory and practice. The changes in capitalism that stem from its existential crisis, we are told, prove that 'we are living in a Marxist moment' (Laffey and Dean 2002: 90). This is an enormously significant statement. Which Marxism? Emmanuel Wallerstein famously refers to a 'thousand Marxisms'. Mark Laffey and Kathryn Dean (2002: 92) describe the difficulty, in the face of a multiplicity of 'Marxisms', of making choices between them. Can the claim that Marxism can address the questions that twenty-first century capitalism faces be taken seriously if it is first necessary to 'choose' between Marxisms?

This dilemma of choice needs to be addressed and resolved if we are to move forward. A suitable starting point is to regard the problem from the perspective of Marx and the Marxist method of analysis. While this has already been discussed, it is worth recalling Marx's (1974) proposition that what was important was to make observations that move from the simple to the complex – from labour, value, exchange and ultimately leading to globalised capitalist relations and the world market. It was the inter-relationship of all component parts that was paramount. What can be observed in much contemporary Marxist theory is an unwillingness to acknowledge those simple truths. Issues of class, exploitation and economics as the engine of political movement are all too often downplayed. Capitalism and its development are predicated on the appropriation of surplus value. Capitalist society is based on the notion of an economic base, upon which rests a political and social superstructure. The state, as facilitator of the dominant economic ideology, is rooted in class and class divisions. These are issues that define Marxism. Ultimately there is one capitalism that essentially conforms to that pattern. It adapts to changes in prevailing conditions as a means of seeking escape from its inherent contradictions but remains the obstacle to emancipation of the working class and its allies. There can, at the end of the day, be only one Marxism capable of issuing a successful challenge to capitalist rule. Contemporary Marxism, to its credit, seeks to answer the questions that capitalism poses. What it has failed to do is to promote a practice that will defeat capitalism.

Capitalism, in the twenty-first century, is mired in crisis. William Tabb (2010: 320) makes an obvious point but one worth remembering that capitalism disregards any interests other than those that serve its development and that this disregard of communities and of the working people is heightened in periods of crisis. Tabb cites Robert Brenner's comments that 'the basic source of today's crisis is the declining vitality of the advanced economies since 1973 and especially since 2000' (2010: 317). Experience shows that crisis, rather than abating, will deepen.

Assessments such as Brenner's, however, do little to resolve the problem. There are any number of voices willing to point out what is wrong. Other voices that consciously call for an active and ideologically charged challenge to capitalist rule, however, remain muted. Capitalism is all too easily let off the hook. When capitalism's excesses become too obvious to ignore then ways and means are employed to mask the worst effects of such excess. As Michael Lebowitz describes, 'new regulations, new limits, new forms of oversight are seen as a solution to abuse and excess...Bad capitalists, rather than capitalism itself are identified as the evil' (2012b: 59). Capitalist crisis has not led to effective challenge. There needs to be a force that can channel the discontent that such crisis creates, but little has been done to resolve the problem. For many, capitalism remains an almost immutable force. Once more we hear the echo of the Luxemburg/Bernstein polemic: reform or revolution? 'Marxism' may make all sorts of claims to an intellectual, moral, analytical high-ground but the words of Luxemburg are still bitingly fresh:

> As long as theoretic knowledge remains the privilege of a handful of 'academicians' in the party, the latter will face the danger of going astray. Only when the great mass of workers take the keen and dependable weapons of scientific socialism in their own hands will all the petty bourgeois inclinations, all the opportunist currents, come to naught. The movement will then find itself on sure and firm ground. 'Quantity will do it' (1982: 10).

Luxemburg's call for 'quantity' appears even more remote than when she uttered those words in 1900, but it need not be so. Influential 'Marxist' theorists of the late twentieth and early twenty-first century have, in their quest to remain 'relevant', weakened the movement that must change the world. There have been many departures from the essence of Marxist theory, but the most telling, from the perspective of presenting a serious challenge to the dominance of capitalism, has been the move away from class as the pivotal issue. At the same time, it must be remembered that there is a continually expanding working class and that this class is being created by capitalism. By 2030 there will be 3.5 billion members of the global working class.

Contemporary Marxist theory promoted the merits of identity politics and social movement politics ahead of the working class. This is despite the obvious fact that there is a vast reservoir of working class potential upon which to draw in the struggle against capitalism. The working class remains the central force for effecting fundamental change. It exists, it has aspirations that are antagonistic to capitalism, and is constantly under threat as the crisis of capitalism continues to deepen. To relegate this force to a position of relative obscurity and insignificance is a position that is, at best, deeply flawed. At the same time, it is an objective reality that social movement politics have the capacity to engage large numbers. Marxist approaches to the issues of twenty-first century capitalism and its crisis need to recognise this. The organisation and leadership of anti-capitalist movements will necessitate a confluence of these two forces, but this can only be achieved by resolving the issue of leadership. Chris Harman depicts the twentieth century as a century of wars, civil wars and revolutions. He argues that this also characterises the twenty-first century. The decisive question, in his view, is 'what forces exist that are capable of taking on the system and transforming the world?' (Harman 1999: 329). It is a question that has been debated for decades. A successful resolution to that question also offers the definitive answer to the question of whether Marxism can address the questions that twenty-first century capitalism poses.

Resolving the crisis in Marxism

Those questions, as to which forces are best suited to bring about change, and the question of leadership are vitally important. They sit alongside another big question that first must be answered. Can the crisis in Marxism be resolved? This is no time to be coy. We need to decide which is the best way forward. Is it in seeking some real or imagined unity between 'Marxisms' or by engaging in ideological struggle that would see a final parting of the ways between contemporary and classical Marxism? At face value it would seem that some form of 'unity ticket' might be possible, but so often, choosing what at first glance seems an obvious or easy option has led many into dark places and blind alleys.

However, let us look at the possibilities of a resolution of the difficulties that separate contemporary Marxist thought from classical Marxism. Surely common ground might be found by simply establishing and isolating core values upon which all can agree. A starting point might be to consider the central contradictions that are observable in capitalism. These include the private nature of ownership and the public nature of the production process, the necessity to globalise economic relations while maintaining a reliance on the nation-state as a political foundation, and the drive to maximise profits and surplus value while facing a tendency to see profit rates fall.

Alarm bells immediately ring even though these contradictions are obvious and self-evident. The first seems safe enough, although the potential for unity becomes a little frayed when the second point is considered. Nationalism and nationalist sentiments, those echoes of a Stalinist past and a vivid reminder of the limitations that so many on the left seem happy to live with, make agreement more than a little unlikely. The theory of the falling rate of profit, the third point, is a stumbling block as so many theorists have long discounted it. When all is said and done, so many of the problems lie in attitudes to economic matters and particularly around the proposition that economic issues drive political outcomes – the base/superstructure thesis. This idea, so central to Marxist theory, remains possibly the most divisive. Even so there are still shared values. Marxism after all is the antithesis of capitalism and offers a thorough analysis of capitalism's trajectory. But is this enough for a resolution of differences? Inevitably, problems arise around the working class and the practice of Marxism, which, after all, exists to displace capitalism and actively promotes the view that the working class is the force that has the potential to overthrow capitalism.

Marxism has, since its formation, been engaged in intense polemic and has always dwelt in a contentious terrain. To expect that the divergent trends within Marxist theory could find common cause or principled unity is unlikely. This observation is not made from a position of pessimism. Marxism offers a rational path to change. The choice of path is what divides Marxism and, paradoxically, offers a means of by-passing rather than resolving the crisis that has so long afflicted Marxist thought.

Describing 'problems' in Marxism, from a Marxist perspective, is nothing new. Georgi Plekhanov (1976), Karl Korsch (1931), the theorists of the Frankfurt School, Western Marxism, the 'New Left', the neo-Marxists, post-Marxists have all focussed on and described the problems. What has become almost commonplace is the claim that the 'crisis is ultimately not one of Marxist philosophy but of Marxism as revolutionary social theory' (McCarney 1990: 189). It is an idea that gained currency as postmodernist and post-Marxist theories developed and an idea that is far removed from anything resembling a Marxist perspective.

Flowing from this are reactions to the Marxist idea of the 'revolutionary potential of the working class'. It is rather important. The working class, regardless of poor leadership, or periods of indifference, remains a potentially revolutionary force. Three interconnected elements validate this proposition. Firstly, the working class is the class that, by its labour, produces and reproduces capitalist production and class relations (Marx 1986a: 529-530). Secondly, the needs of opposing classes remain intensely contradictory (Marx and Engels 1977: 35-36). Finally, the working class has become an increasingly globalised class as capitalism itself has become a globalised economic structure (Silver 2006). Recognition of these three facts becomes pivotal when considering the prospects for Marxism.

Class formation, in Marx's view, had little to do with aspirations or desires. 'Men make their own history, but they do not make it just as they please; they do not make it under circumstances chosen by themselves, but under circumstances directly encountered, given and transmitted from the past' (Marx 1986e: 97). It is a view that needs to be considered in the light of much contemporary Marxist scholarship. 'Identification' with a group, rather than a place in a set of economic arrangements, has become the dominant idea. The role and potential power of the working class has been diminished within the broad scope of what is a defeatist theory.

The issue of class and the role of the working class continues to be among the most vexatious in terms of finding any elusive 'common ground' among Marxists. Despite evidence to the contrary (Silver 2006, World Bank 1995, Dobbs *et al* 2012) some 'Marxist' analysts still maintain that a global 'proletarianisation' has not occurred and it is unlikely that it will do so (Sitton 2010: 15). Sitton does not deny that struggles against capital are a fact of life. He argues that:

> Multiple forces of opposition are gathering in the world today. Some are trying to protect their jobs, their culture, the environment, or their families. Others are simply asserting human dignity in the face of crushing circumstance. Overthrow by a self-conscious proletariat has never been the only possibility...whatever their motives, they will be determined that economies exist to serve people, not people to serve economies (2010: 26).

Reform or revolution? What to do with the working class? These same nagging and irksome problems remain for far too many theorists. There remains an odd reluctance to acknowledge the potential power of the working class. At the same time the need for 'change' is broadly accepted. Fuentes-Ramirez (2014: 142), for instance, argues that change can be brought about by influencing the state to empower institutions that might, in turn, cause 'ruptures' within capitalist institutions. To separate state institutions from capitalist institutions and to use one set against another would seem an unlikely scenario. David Harvey (2012: xiii) shifts the focus again when he speaks of a revolutionary working class being constituted from urban rather than 'exclusively' factory workers. Harvey argues that 'glimmers' of hope are visible. He bases these hopes on the left-populist movements in Spain and Greece and on what he describes as 'revolutionary impulses' in Latin America (2012: 157). Unfortunately, history can move at great speed. Harvey's 'glimmers' are now very faint indeed. Harvey's argument was strongly influenced by the *Occupy Wall Street Movement*. Once more there is a problem. The Occupy movement came and went, leaving barely a ripple on the surface. He proposes that the anti-capitalist movement should connect with the alienated and discontented and that this 'movement' 'be democratically assembled into a coherent opposition...an alternative political system, and, ultimately, an alternative way of organizing production, distribution, and consumption for the benefit of the people' (Harvey 2012: 162-163). While recognising the need to effect change and even 'revolutionary' change, two factors remain obscure and understated. How is this change to be brought about and which forces will bring about change? They are questions that go to the heart of any real chance for Marxist realignment or resolution to the theoretical differences within Marxist theory. The potential for realigning Marxist theory, or of resolving the differences within Marxist theory, must be seriously considered if Marxism is to fulfil its historical role. None of capitalism's historical contradictions have been resolved but, rather, have become more acute.

Contemporary Marxist theory remains divided and limited when discussing anything akin to a unity of purpose between theory and practice. However, issues at the heart of Marxism, the working class and its identification as revolutionary subject, must remain at the centre of both theory and practice. To do otherwise is to continue to diminish and disarm Marxism, and, in turn, the working class. We need to be frank. While there might be areas of accord, a common approach will not become a reality. There is too much that divides the 'thousand Marxisms' and there is too much at stake. This might sound melodramatic, but not when considered in the light of the crisis of capitalism, of the threats that this crisis presents to the planet and to the working people. The people need better than chaos and uncertainty. While consensus will not be found, the polemic remains just as important, or possibly even more important than ever. Ideas matter and the battle of ideas strengthens theory and ultimately can strengthen practice.

The crisis in Marxist theory can be resolved but not at any price and certainly not at the price of abandoning the theory that can offer serious challenge. Which forces, then, are most likely to bring about change?

Getting things straight

The moment the question arises about which forces might transform the world, the wheel again spins, bringing us straight back to issues of class and social identity. Enough has been said concerning the inadequacies of identity politics. This issue must be finally resolved if we are to navigate a meaningful way out of the morass and to combat capitalism.

Class, as far as Marx was concerned, was the foundation-stone of economic and political structures. That needs to be borne in mind. The 'history of all hitherto existing society is the history of class struggles' (Marx and Engels 1977: 35). Class identification ought not be a tricky thing, but it has become so. In the 1990s less than half of all Australians were prepared to even acknowledge that they belonged to any class. Such has been the success of the ideological fog machine of the state. Figures from the United States (Newport 2015) show that identification with the working class has risen rapidly in direct proportion to the rise of inequality. This is significant. Class does matter and especially when the crisis of capitalism becomes more visibly acute.

While class identification may be a subjective thing, a Marxist understanding of class is not. At its simplest, class can be determined by where one lines up in relation to the ownership of the means of production, distribution and exchange. 'It is always the direct relationship of the owners of the conditions of production to the direct producers' (Marx 1986b: 791). Marx elaborated on this, differentiating between 'the owners merely of labour-power, owners of capital, and landowners, whose respective sources of income are wages, profit and ground-rent, in other words, wage-labourers, capitalists, and landlords, constitute then three big classes of modern society based upon the capitalist mode of production' (Marx 1986b: 885). Such divisions cannot help but be antagonistic and constitute the basis of the concept of class consciousness as well as social inequality.

A class-based society and economy inevitably leads to inequality and, importantly, to an awareness of inequality. Marx used the analogy of a house to describe this sense of awareness:

> A house may be large or small; as long as the surrounding houses are equally small it satisfies all social demands for a dwelling. But let a palace arise beside the little house, and it shrinks from a little house to a hut...the occupant of the relatively small house will feel more and more uncomfortable, dissatisfied and cramped within its four walls (1986e: 83).

This has become so 'natural' as to be ignored and taken for granted. What has happened, over time, has been a concerted and successful ideological offensive waged by capitalism and the state. It has, by falsely building a sense of national unity and common cause, magnificently fostered a belief among many that there are shared interests based not on class, but on national identity. It is but a short step from national identity to a social identity. So successful has this been that many activists and theorists alike have sought to construct a framework that advantages identity over class. We may like it or not, but non-class and supra-class approaches to capitalism enjoy a position of dominance and, as such, need to be seriously considered.

Identity politics theorists can become a little intoxicated by their own rhetoric. Some go so far as to claim that their theory has become the only 'valid' response to inequality (Castells 2004: 11-12). Disturbingly Manuel Castells informs us that the 'ideological emptiness created by the failure of Marxism-Leninism to actually indoctrinate the masses was replaced, in the 1980s, when people were able to express themselves, by the only source of identity... in the collective memory: *national identity*' (2004: 43, italics in the original). Ignoring the hubris for a moment, it remains that for large numbers of people, identity has become central. If Castells is correct, then the sources of inequality ought to have been identified, organised against, challenged and, by sheer dint of the 'superiority' of the theory, inequality ought to be declining rather than rising so sharply.

What needs to be remembered is that those who maintain an anti-capitalist perspective *may* share an identity but they *do* share a class. To deny class is to ignore the magnitude of the billions-strong global working class and, in large measure, to ignore Marxism. The two are inseparable. To weaken one, weakens the other. Michael Lebowitz (2004) makes an obvious but compelling point that capitalism's ability to 'keep going', or to reproduce itself, is due in large part to the acquiescence of the working class. He speaks of a dependency that workers feel for capitalism. They come to believe that capitalism meets their needs and that the worker needs capitalism:

> As long as workers have not broken with the idea that capital is necessary, a state under their control will act to facilitate the conditions for the reproduction of capital...Capitalism produces the working class it needs. It produces workers who look upon it as necessary...A system where the reproduction of capital is necessary for the reproduction of wage laborers.

What keeps capitalism going? Wage laborers (2004: 24).

Capitalism requires an exploited working class to survive. This is a *necessity*. A working class that is divided across often arbitrary lines of race, gender, ethnicity and sexuality becomes *useful* for capitalism. Resolving any of these non-class issues would not undermine the rule of capitalism to the slightest degree.

Which forces, then, are most likely to bring about real and fundamental change? Marxist theory was built upon the premise that an organised working class is central to challenging capitalism. The development of class consciousness and organisation of the working class is not something that happens spontaneously. A degree of coyness exists when describing this channelling of discontent. The organisational structure that would seem to be inevitable under conditions of class rule is an overtly political organisation – a political party – framed by Marxist theory. The reluctance of many Marxists to speak in terms of political organisation is understandable. The history of Marxist political parties throughout the twentieth century has been mired in Stalinism. Non-Stalinist Marxist political expressions have been dogged by problems associated with perceived irrelevance that afflict small and often powerless organisations. To speak, therefore, of a Marxist party that might organisationally arm the working class is often derided, but any movement that might challenge the rule of capital can only be an organised one. Organisational structures for today and beyond therefore need some consideration. Central to this is to find ways to overcome what is best described as an on-going crisis of leadership.

Out of the darkness

If, then, the working class is the force that will challenge capitalism and replace it, then how is it to go about the task? So much has been put into place by the state to ensure that this most dangerous class is kept submissive and acquiescent. Capitalism is, in the eyes of the majority of the working class, something that is almost unchangeable. It seems to have always existed and we are told, almost on a daily basis, that there is no alternative and that if something goes wrong, then it can be fixed. If socialism is not just to be considered an option, but a real option to be fought for, then serious questions need to be addressed. How is the working class to find out about this real option and of its merits? How is it going to organise itself, if not through the old nationally-based organisations that are now a part of the state? What then are the best means to achieve what seems to be such a mammoth task? If we can satisfactorily answer these questions, then we will be well on the way to resolving the problems facing the people.

A lot of words have been uttered, arguing why the working class is or is not the major component in the cause for change, but Trotsky, in one sentence, summed up the situation. 'The world political situation as a whole is chiefly characterized by a historical crisis of the leadership of the proletariat' (1977: 1). Obviously, he had more to say than this, but it serves to illustrate both the simplicity and depth of the task before those who would seek a better future. Trotsky's use of prose was clear and to the point.

The last few decades have seen many of the theorists of contemporary Marxism despatching the working class to some nether world. How socialism is to replace capitalism without the working class is tricky enough. How to wage any form of political struggle against capitalism is another and it too has been handled with indecision and confusion. Many of these theorists can clearly state what it is that they don't want (capitalism) and many can state what it is that they do want (socialism) but are left to wanting or wishing or hoping that sometime, somehow, things will turn out for the best.

So many theorists who seek to find a way forward recognise

that socialism needs to be the ultimate destination and that the levels of discontent are growing at the same pace that social equality is disappearing. Werner Bonefeld (2006) is just one who questions the capacity of anti-capitalist, anti-globalisation movements if they do not espouse a socialist alternative. Responses are frequently conflicting. Harvey writes that:

> there is no resolute and sufficiently unified anti-capitalist movement that can adequately challenge the reproduction of the capitalist class and the perpetuation of its power on the world stage...but just because there is no political force capable of articulating let alone mounting such a program, this is no reason to hold back on outlining alternatives (2010: 250).

This certainly sounds encouraging, but then a degree of apprehension quickly emerges. Harvey goes on to argue for what he describes as a 'co-revolutionary' theory to build opposition to capitalism, concluding his appeal by effectively dismissing Marxist organisational 'party' structures. Instead he retreats into a pleasant but impossible dream, claiming that while 'traditional institutionalized communism is as good as dead and buried, there are...millions of de facto communists active among us, willing to act upon their understandings, ready to creatively pursue anti-capitalist imperatives' (Harvey 2010: 260). Just what these 'understandings' may be might vary dramatically. How an individual is to act on these 'understandings' remains a mystery. What is clearly lacking, but what is required, is a leadership that can develop and unite disparate forces and ideas into a movement that can effectively challenge and defeat capitalism.

Without such a leadership, the actions of the many who are drawn into activity are ultimately in vain. Capitalism and its structures remain intact. Capitalism and the state can accommodate such actions and even portray them as indications of the 'health' of society. While there is an objective necessity to confront capitalism, capitalist ideology and a weakness in much that constitutes contemporary Marxist theory combines to obscure that very need. This is by no means a new phenomenon. Marx, over 160 years ago, wrote in his *Address of the Central Committee to the Communist League* that 'the democratic petty bourgeois, far from wanting to transform the whole society in the interests of the revolutionary proletarians, only aspire to a change in social conditions which will make the existing society as tolerable and comfortable for themselves as possible' (cited in D'Amato 2006: 104).

While there is a reluctance to consider how change can be implemented there is no shortage of calls for a different future. Alain Badiou typifies these, often amorphous, calls to the future:

> The communist hypothesis is that a different collective organization is practicable, one that will eliminate the inequality of wealth and even the division of labour. The private appropriation of massive fortunes and their transmission by inheritance will disappear. The existence of a coercive state, separate from civil society, will no longer appear a necessity: a long process of reorganization based on a free association of producers will see it withering away (2008: 42).

It all sounds, at least at face value, rather good. There is certainly a desire to break from capitalism and a wish for 'something better'. What is less evident is how to go about it. There is a reluctance to talk about the paths to that desired future. This is perfectly understandable. Political organisation that focuses directly on replacing capitalism is associated in the collective memory to the politics of Stalinist parties, to authoritarianism, to curtailing of individual freedoms and to oppressive and repressive party structures. As it was when the stain of Stalinism first seeped into the Marxist movement, when Stalinism was equated with Marxism, so too today, contemporary Marxist theorists, in seeking to 'rescue' Marxism, would unwittingly consign it to obscurity and irrelevance, leaving capitalism to continue lurching from crisis to crisis and to wreak havoc upon the people and the planet.

It is as though these theorists have become 'caught in the headlights' and can move neither forward nor backward. It is hard to imagine something better, something different, something that could and would work, but it is not an impossible task, especially as history offers more than hints at the way forward. It is, in fact, a fear of failure or of replicating failure of the past. Consequently, the theorists, it would seem, can go so far and no farther. Eric Swyngedouw describes the situation whereby the 'fear of failing has become so overwhelming that fear of real change is all that is left; resistance is as far as our horizons reach – transformation, it seems, can no longer be thought, let alone practiced' (2010: 317). However, even while acknowledging the problem that 'fear' remains, he still fails to move beyond the call, in principle at least, for change. This 'revolutionary' change requires two conditions to occur. Productive forces need to be highly developed and the working class and its allies must assume political power. In other words, what is required is a coming together of objective and subjective conditions for fundamental change. The objective conditions for fundamental change are well in place and have been for some time. The subjective factors – the class consciousness of the working class as revolutionary subject armed with a resolute political leadership – remain in embryonic form.

Into the light

Classical Marxist literature, or rather the words of those early Marxists – Marx, Engels, Lenin, Trotsky, Luxemburg and the rest – share a pithy, simple and accessible style. Perhaps it was because they were writing for a specific audience and knew their audience well. They were writing for workers and all had the ability to quickly 'cut to the chase'. It is an observation worth contemplating when thinking about organisational structures for the future.

To move forward means overcoming the 'crisis of leadership' that so clearly exists. The working class is the class most capable of bringing about fundamental change. This requires a high degree of class consciousness – socialist consciousness. This consciousness needs to be guided to action that will result in both a challenge to capitalism and to its replacement as a ruling idea. The most obvious form of such leadership is one based in Marxist theory and practice. This is best represented in that special form of political organisation, the Marxist party.

If capitalism is to be confronted, then it is obvious that there needs to be a way of preparing for and organising that confrontation. Historical moments have arisen when change might have been achieved and yet capitalism remains the obviously dominant paradigm. The failures of the working-class movement can be attributed, as Trotsky (1974) forcefully did, to a failure of leadership of the working class. The earliest 'failures' following the 1917 Russian Revolution have a common denominator. The German revolution of 1923, the Chinese revolution of 1925-27, the British General Strike of 1926, the Spanish Civil War are all testimony to the anti-Marxism that epitomised Stalinist theory and practice. If there are any lingering doubts, the rise of Hitler needs to be borne in mind. It was a resistible rise but the politics of the Comintern saw the German working class divided and the rest, as they say, is a blood-stained history. All of this led to a feeling of despair as to any benefit that an organised party might possess. Most parties had become Stalinist. Therefore, in the minds of many, party organisation equated with Stalinist methods.

The realities that confront the world and the global working class in the twenty-first century, however, make it necessary to rethink, to abandon the past and to finally remove the stain of Stalin. There is a clear need of a political movement that has consistent and independent leadership. It is too much to expect that the working class alone can develop a socialist consciousness by some sort of political osmosis. It has long been an accepted truth in Marxism that socialist consciousness develops both within the working class but significantly from forces working with the working class who develop the theory that will inform practice. This is a long and arduous process that cannot be subject to the rises and falls that so often mark out more spontaneous activities. This is certainly the case in relation to the actions of identity and social movement politics. It is also an imperative that such a political expression is based on an internationalist perspective and has nothing to do with the promotion of nationalist responses to global questions.

Marx and Engels (1977: 49) were clear in their estimation that the essence of a communist organisation is that it operates in the interests of the working class, regardless of nationality and in the direct interests of the movement as a whole. For them, emancipation and the challenge to capitalism was, necessarily, to be organised through a political organisation and this organisation could only be a political party organised at the global level. This is even more relevant today as capitalism has assumed an intensely global character. The significance of Marxism in the era of capitalist crisis lies in its insistence upon its organisational capacity, its internationalism, its analytical abilities and a capacity to merge theory and practice.

For progress to be made, the working class must be returned to a position of centrality. Marxism has long worked for a political movement of the working class as the most appropriate means of leading a movement that seeks to change the world. This is why Marx and Engels wrote the *Manifesto of the Communist Party* as a guide to the embryonic *Communist League*.

Patience is required but is sometimes sorely tried. John Sitton laments that Marx never 'clarified what would be the form of the proletariat organized as the ruling class' (2010: 12). It is a curious, if not baffling, lament. All too often classical Marxists are falsely attacked for regarding Marx's words as something akin to 'holy writ' and yet these attackers, when it suits, seem to demand that a prescriptive formula for change be presented. Marxists in a capitalist world can, justifiably, seek to create the conditions by which such a transformation might be enacted, but not determine what and how that future society would operate. The role and purpose of such a party in the twenty-first century is central to clarifying what Marxism is 'for' in this century, its claim to relevance and what forces are best suited to promote the emancipatory project of the working class.

What that form of political organisation takes is necessarily dependent upon the objective conditions that exist. What is clear is that the essential formation of any such political organisation cannot be limited by national boundaries and nor could it hope to exist under the 'patronage' of the state that it ultimately would seek to challenge. John Rees argues that:

> A revolutionary organization remains the indispensable tool...Without the struggle to build such an organization, the danger remains that the dialectic of capitalist development will remain...but if the struggle to build such an organization is successful, we have a chance – not more, not less – to make the leap from the realm of necessity to the realm of freedom (1998: 301-302).

It is around this 'call to arms' that Marxism, in the age of capitalist crisis, can assert its relevance and discover ways to resolve the crisis that has been a feature of its development for the better part of a century.

The concept of working-class political organisations that

move beyond the limitations of national borders is an area that deserves special and urgent attention. The period of Stalinism and the negative experience of Marxist political parties, both as ruling parties and as working-class parties in the capitalist world, has had a lasting and negative legacy. This is evident from within Marxist theory and from the point of view of many within the broad working-class and anti-capitalist movements. Feelings of antipathy towards political parties that proclaim themselves to be Marxist are entirely understandable when considered against the backdrop of recent history, and yet it is in the realm of political activity that an alternative to capitalist rule can best be envisaged.

There is an undeniable need of political organisation among the working class that could offer a real challenge to the rule of capital. The collapse of the USSR and its 'fraternal' political organisations around the world was heralded by many as marking the death knell of organised Marxist politics. A contrary perspective is that with the passing of Stalinism and the false perception that it represented a legitimate expression of Marxism, a potential exists for a rebuilding of the idea of Marxist political organisation within the working class movement. This, by implication, would occupy a different terrain to that of its predecessors and would necessarily be a global organisation operating in a unified manner across states. This formulation closely resembles that of the Third International before it became Stalinised and the continuation of that model as represented by Trotsky's Fourth International.

There are any number of 'revolutionary', 'communist', 'socialist' parties, all laying claim to be Marxist. A Marxist party that could change the world must recognise certain truths and these truths must be recognised by those who might seek a political expression. Capitalism can only survive by exploiting the working class. The interests of the working class and those of the ruling class are fundamentally opposed. Class, therefore, is important. Capitalism can only be defeated by an economic and political struggle by the working class with a political and theoretical leadership that comes from Marxism. Political campaigns based on race, ethnicity, gender, sexuality or any variant of identity politics can never be expected to challenge the rule of capital. No amount of reform will threaten capitalism. No identity-based campaign, no social movement, can ever be as powerful as the working class. The global working class is counted in the billions. The working class has traditionally been organised politically by social-democratic parties and economically by the trade unions. These organisations, it must be remembered, became integrated into the state. The parties of social democracy do not threaten the state because they are institutions of the state. The unions do not threaten the state because they have become institutions of that same state. Under such conditions the working class can have no capacity for independent action. The only path for independent activity for the working class can be through a political party that explicitly seeks to challenge capitalism. Capital is a global force. It does not recognise national borders. The working class, too, is a global force but is trapped into a perspective that is bound up in nationalist symbolism. A political struggle against a global enemy can, therefore, only be waged on a global battleground. Most parties that adopt the names of 'revolutionary', or 'socialist' or 'Marxist' tend not to recognise those truths. This is not to say that such an alternative does not exist, but it does suggest that the 'buyer' needs to beware.

In order to change the world, there must be a close interplay between theory and practice. Alvin Gouldner (1980: 1-7) describes the coming to power of the Bolsheviks in 1917, highlighting the importance of a theoretical underpinning of revolutionary practice. Anton Pannekoek, writing during World War I and on the eve of the 1917 Revolution, stated what was, for Marxists, an unarguable reality. 'Man is only the agent of economic needs;

but these needs can only be changed thanks to his activity. Both parts are equally correct and important, and together they form a complete theory' (Pannekoek 1915). Marxism remains a philosophy that is integrally and dialectically connected to the economy. It is a philosophy that is fundamentally connected to the world, while simultaneously seeking to change and construct a new world.

Despite the best efforts of the capitalist nation-state and despite the distortions of Marxism by so many contemporary Marxist theoreticians, the ideas first propounded by Marx and Engels and advanced by classical Marxists still hold the attention of millions around the world. With the stain of Stalinism being cleared from Marxism, and with capitalism ever more deeply mired in crisis, socialism is once more on the agenda and in the thoughts of many. The opinion polls referred to a little earlier are one indicator of this. Another simple fact remains. One little book, the *Manifesto of the Communist Party*, remains defiantly in print 170 years after first appearing. It is read in 200 languages and, in 2015, when Penguin brought out its Little Black Classics, featuring 80 classic titles, the *Manifesto* was by far its best seller. Why? The answer is in the message that the book, and Marxism, delivers. It bodes well for the future and for the promise of Marxism, no longer stained by Stalinism.

Chapter 7

Conclusion

'Communism is a terrible thing and can never be anything but a terrible thing. Now, Marx and communism, they are very different things. Marx was a revolutionary and stood for social justice. Communism is the opposite.'

It was one of those unexpected moments. A chance comment to a stranger reading a book on a park bench led to a sharing of what people were reading. The stranger was reading Steinbeck. Another was reading Tolstoy. From Tolstoy, the conversation moved, apparently quite logically to Russia and from there to the adamant claim that communism was a 'terrible thing'. While the 'point' was clumsily made, it remains a commonly held view. At least Marx was not being held guilty for the 'crimes' of communism. All too often Marx is seen as an almost evil progenitor, whose blood-line ends with Stalin. The encounter took place only hours before I began writing this concluding chapter. Timing, as they say, is everything.

The book began with a simple statement of intent. It was neither a warning, nor an apology, but referred to a reality that informs our thinking. It simply signposted what was to come, that the book was about ideas and about the battle of ideas. We all of us live in and around this world of ideas. For the most part it is framed by the ruling ideology and in this case the ideology is 'bourgeois'. It cannot be anything else. The ruling ideology is inevitably linked to the ruling economic and political idea. That statement of intent was clear as to the partisanship nature of what was to follow. Sides were being taken and positions being taken in that battle of ideas. The arguments that were to follow were against the continued rule of capital, and for socialism, for Marxism, but not just any socialism and definitely not just any

'Marxism'. In this respect the discussion that followed set out to deliberately challenge many of the conceptions of what it is to be anti-capitalist, pro-socialist and even Marxist in the twenty-first century. Not everybody will agree with what has been said, but that does not mean that things must not or should not be said.

The main argument was that Marxism, as an ideological force, established to lead the charge against capitalism, has been poorly served in the past century and that many of its core messages have been obscured. This was not done by Marxism's most obvious ideological foe, capitalism, but rather by voices that speak in the name of Marxism. I have described this as a crime, although it is doubtful that those 'charged' acted with criminal intent. Two separate but interrelated forces have, unwittingly, assisted capitalism's rule and allowed it to lurch from crisis to crisis without offering anything like serious combat. The first force was Stalinism. Successive 'Marxists' in trying to rescue the theory from Stalinism have only served to weaken Marxism and the working class, the class that Marxism was formed to arm.

The book has made no claim to be a once and for all answer and model for a renewed Marxism that will lead the working class. That is the work for many minds and many activists. It simply set itself the task of taking part in an important discussion, of defending Marxism and of placing the concept of the working class at the centre of struggle. It focussed on the damage done to Marxism, in the name of Marxism, of the core values of its theory that have been relegated to insignificance by successive generations of 'Marxist' theoreticians, and of the necessity to link theory to a practice that will serve the working class. It also outlined the need for new organisational structures that can re-arm the working class. It argued that the only way for any of this to eventuate is for the stain of Stalinism to be finally removed and for a political projection of Marxism to become a global reality.

What went wrong?

Socialism has not overcome capitalism. That is obvious. Something went very wrong on the way from first presenting a critique of capitalism, to formulating a theory that would provide an understanding of capitalism and allow for a practice that would defeat capitalism. To suggest otherwise would be naïve in the extreme. It would be foolish, however, to imagine that capitalism has anything positive to offer. Its moment in time has passed. This is clear to all. It is equally clear that there are millions, hundreds of millions of people whose lives are negatively impacted by capitalism's continuing and deepening crisis. People are increasingly being made aware of where the problem lies. However, it is not enough to know what is wrong and to simply wish for something better. 'Marxist' theory, in the past century, has produced an almost endless set of critiques, but apart from well-intentioned hand-wringing, has failed to move beyond describing what is wrong.

Contemporary Marxism has, unwittingly, aided and abetted the continuation of capitalism by inaction and paralysis. Each 'new' development in the realm of theory has meant another step away from the essence and core values of Marxism. It is no difficult thing to sit on the sidelines and throw stones at these theoreticians. Their actions, as I have sought to explain, were not made from intentional malice, but from a series of small steps leading away from those core elements. It has ended in a trajectory that has effectively rejected Marx, the working class, and has led to despair, despondency and defeatism.

This was, as the book explains, not a product of this or that wrong approach but has its roots deeply embedded in responses to a far greater and more malignant problem. That problem was, of course, Stalinism. Marxism was confronted with a dilemma of mammoth proportions. What to do about Stalinism? For some it was acquiescence and betrayal. These forces went along with the distortions and mutations of theory and the abandonment of revolutionary practice to better suit the requirements of Stalinism and its nationalist perspectives. For others it was a mission of 'rescue' of Marxism that led to the erosion of theory and practice that is evidenced by social movement and identity politics at the expense of the working class. For some, however, and these represented a tiny minority, the challenge was to 'stick' with Marx and the ideology of classical Marxism.

Tracing these various courses has been at the centre of this work. There is a danger, however, in being simply dismissive of any opposing voice. Overcoming that temptation should sit at the heart of any polemic. This book is something of an extended polemic. It is certainly critical and highly critical of those theorists who have served Marxism so poorly, but also set itself the task of offering something positive in return. In this sense the book remains optimistic. It sees the future as being bright.

The work set itself some very specific tasks, but there remained, at heart, a call to optimism. For some that might seem ridiculous, given the state of the world and the despair, atomisation and defeatism that abounds. There are, of course, limitations to any work such as this, not the least of which is the sheer magnitude of the task itself. I have argued for Marxism as a way out of the morass, but this can easily become just another case of wishing for something better, hoping that one day, somehow, all will work out for the best. If that were the case, then it would have been better had this book not been written. Clearly, one book, one set of thoughts, is not about to change the mindsets of the many. It is only one voice that plays, at best, a tiny part in poking the consciousness, the imaginations of those who are most at risk from capitalism.

Any movement for serious change must explore what needs to be done. There is a movement, a philosophy, a theory that is already intact and in place. The book first explained what went wrong and why. What followed was a serious exploration of how to recapture momentum and to discover what 'excess baggage' might be jettisoned in order to assist forward motion.

The need to 'de-clutter'

The decades following the 1917 Revolution and the subsequent Stalinisation of Marxism were decades of theoretical searching for ways to re-invigorate Marxism. What transpired was quite the opposite. Each step along the path to making Marxism 'relevant' in the face of this or that crisis seemed to mean exchanging Marxist theory for something less. Along the way, the working class and its potential to challenge capital was relegated to insignificance. Class politics was replaced with the politics of identity. Any central focus on economic issues as having a central role was equally disregarded. For some, Marx and Engels were no longer presented as inseparable allies but as mutually antagonistic characters. Internationalism was exchanged for a return to nationalism, albeit of a 'left' populist variety. The concept of the Marxist party came into serious question, to be replaced with spontaneity and claims that there were millions of 'de facto' communists who would, presumably, act independently of any 'authoritarian' structures. In short, a whole lot of baggage was collected along the way. There were just fading glimpses to be seen of the Marxism that 'shook the world' in 1917. There is nothing, it would seem, all that new under the sun. Many years ago, Lenin cuttingly reproached those that would lead the movement into the 'marsh'. He wrote that, 'you are free not only to invite us, but to go yourselves wherever you will, even into the marsh' (1977d: 97-98). Those that he was criticising were not deliberately setting about to 'harm' the movement, but their actions led Lenin to that conclusion. The point has more than a little in common with the 'baggage-collectors' of the twentieth and early twenty-first century.

Classical Marxism, if it is to be taken seriously and to deserve its claim to optimism, cannot shy away from these truths, not so dissimilar to those confronted by Lenin. The excess baggage must be shed. The 'clutter' must be sorted out. There is little hope of running some unity ticket with Wallerstein's 1000 Marxisms. It was in this combative spirit that the book sought to examine the range of theories and practices that have been presented in the name of 'anti-capitalist' struggle in the last several decades. Capitalism has not been challenged and it cannot be challenged by calls to identity, to campaigns based in and around issues of race, identity, ethnicity, gender or sexuality. They are issues that can be resolved and tackled by many forces but resolving any or all of them will not weaken the rule of capitalism. The book strenuously argued for a return to the core values and motivations that drove Marxism to political action.

Removing 'clutter' is important. It allows us to focus on what is important. It also forces us to consider the foundations and to check whether they are firm. In this case the foundations of Marxism remain intact. Damage has been done. Stalinism has so distorted the theory as to leave so many believing that there is a genealogical link between Marx and Stalin. The victims in all of this are the working class, who deserve so much more than is offered by contemporary Marxist theory and practice.

The foundations are still strong

The point was made that it is not good enough to simply rail against what you might see as wrong. It is easy to be *against* things. I have argued *for* something as well. That 'something' is a return to the core values, the basic assumptions that underpin Marxist theory. Such a proposition might be criticised as being simplistic or naïve. We have all heard it said often enough. It is, after all, a well-worn way of dismissing views that do not sit comfortably, and rather than engaging with an idea, it is simply massaged away. However, the ideas that frame Marxist theory are simple ones. Those that have 'messed' with the theory for the past century have made it virtually incomprehensible.

The clarity of the message becomes dimmed and the 'choice' of which strand of Marxism to follow further clouds the message. Which current of Marxism, which school, which thread is to be followed? Is it to be Western, or libertarian, or structural or cultural, or analytical Marxism? Perhaps it might be neo-Marxism, or Marxist Humanism, or Marxist Feminism or even post-Marxist Marxism. The analysis of classical Marxists has been devalued by these schools of thought. Each strand becomes more and more obtuse, less readable, and ultimately confusing. Things no longer make sense.

We are often told, I have been told, by those who ought to know better, that Marxism is no longer relevant, that the working-class movement is no longer relevant and that the ideas that sprang so clearly from the pages of the *Manifesto* are merely the noble thoughts of a long-dead philosopher and economist. Logic, and the rapidity with which life and experience shows, tells me that such an outlook is one based on confusion and despair. If the complexity of the arguments of latter-day Marxists means that the message has been lost, then perhaps the message needs to be re-stated, in all of its simplicity. Such was the thinking behind this book.

Consequently, the essential elements that constitute a classical Marxist framework were outlined and defended. These included the idea of the base/superstructure description of how capitalism and the state is arranged, with primacy being given to economic structures that inform social and political responses. I stressed the importance of class and of the antagonistic nature of a class-based society, and of the singular importance of the working class in combatting capitalist rule. Marxism's call to internationalism and against any form of nationalist response was also identified as a core element of Marxist theory.

All of these values have been sidelined, diminished and ignored by Stalinist theory and the subsequent 'saviours' of Marxism. At the same time, the book argues that capitalism, as it lurches from crisis to crisis, has been forced to change, not its nature, but its relationships. This was shown through its need to rapidly globalise and to integrate its economic structures while maintaining the nation-state as a means of maintaining a semblance of normality and order.

The case for classical Marxism as a means of explaining the world was vigorously defended.

However, it was argued that the purpose of Marxism is much more than a mechanism by which to explain the world. As a defence of Marxism, the book needed to go a step further. It needed to offer a way forward. In doing so, it adopted an essentially optimistic tone. The future need not be a repeat of the past or a continuation of the present. After all, if all there is to look forward to is a continuation of capitalist crisis and a growing sense of isolation, alienation, insecurity and inequality, then the future would be bleak and intensely depressing. On the contrary, it has been argued that the future can, with work, be a bright one.

A brighter future

Marxism's purpose lies in both explaining and changing the world. It is in this latter part of the aphorism that this work becomes relevant. I have argued for a new way to engage in struggle, or to be more precise, a return to a format that does work. Marx and Engels wrote the *Communist Manifesto*, with a particular purpose in mind. They were operating in an environment that was intensely political. That book was to be used by the Communist League, as a means of motivating and developing a revolutionary understanding that could be turned into revolutionary practice. For them the issue was clear-cut. They had no confusion as to the forces that were best suited to the task. The Communist League, the First International, might have had a short life, but its internationalism was never in question. It existed to organise the working class, regardless of nationality, to wage struggle against capitalism that was already moving beyond the narrow confines of the nation-state. Subsequent organisations, the Second, Third and Fourth Internationals all shared this vision, and all shared an organisational structure. A political expression was to be developed that was international in scope.

This internationalist movement was derailed to serve the nationalist interests of Stalinism in the years following the 1917 revolution. With the passing of time, Stalinism entrenched its hold on the organised working-class movements and Stalinist and non-Stalinist movements alike became increasingly integrated into the structures and institutions of the state. 'Marxist' responses to Stalinism, rather than focussing on the key elements that made Marxism, well, Marxist, did just the opposite, reacting to changes and crises without offering effective leadership. The working-class movement, the Marxist movement, the anti-capitalist movement, all fell into a deep morass of paralysis.

This, it has been shown, unwittingly assisted capitalism to survive its own fundamental and crippling contradictions. I used the rather emotive term 'crime' on more than one occasion. The chief criminal in all of this remains Stalinism. It cast a shadow that still lingers. Its stain remains. All of this might seem a little demoralising. It would be except for a series of interconnected things. These have all formed the basis of the arguments that drive this work. The first thing is that capitalism, impelled by its need to maintain profitability, has rapidly globalised and integrated its relations. This has highlighted the final contradiction of capital. That contradiction being between a globalised economy and the need to maintain the nation-state. Capitalist globalisation has de-industrialised much of the developed world, while developing a huge working class in the developing economies.

Capitalism, in reaching out in such a manner, increases the

capacity for reaction and action. There was, even as this book was being written, an almost historical resurgence of working-class activity across the globe. The US has seen significant working-class unrest, the largest in decades. Tens of thousands of Mexican auto-workers, hundreds of thousands of Indian government workers, South African miners, Zimbabwean teachers, thousands of Belgian postal, hospital, rail and transport workers, Taiwanese pilots and the 'French Yellow' vest protests are all signs of a deepening hostility. This list is hardly exhaustive.

The working class has not gone away, despite oft-repeated claims to the contrary, and neither has Marxism. The book argued that these forces hold the key to a better future. It also vigorously argued that a political expression, through a Marxist party, was an essential requirement. Objectively, capitalism has served its purpose. It can survive only so long as the working class remains without consistent and independent leadership. It is, in the final analysis, not capitalism that bars the way. The obstacle remains the stain of Stalinism. When strangers meet in a park and discuss what they are reading, and the conversation ends up with something like, 'Marx was a revolutionary, his ideas, of socialism and communism, are worth-while,' then we can be confident that the stain has been removed.

Bibliography

Amin, S Hardt, M Lundberg, C Wennerhag, M 2002 'How Capitalism Went Senile' *Eurozine April* Retrieved 22 June 2019 http://www.eurozine.com/articles/2002-05-08-amin-en.html

Anderson, C 1974 *The Political Economy of Social Class*, Prentice Hall Inc., New Jersey

Anderson, P 1979 *Considerations on Western Marxism*, Verso, London

Anderson, P 1998 *The Origins of Postmodernity*, Verso, London

Badiou A 2008 'The communist hypothesis' *New Left Review*, vol. 49, Jan-Feb: 29–42

Bello, W 2004 *Deglobalization: Ideas for a New World Economy*, Zed Books

Berberoglu, B 2009 *Class and Class Conflict in the Age of Globalization*, Lexington Books, Plymouth, UK

Bereciatru, GJ 1994 *Decline of the Nation-State*, University of Nevada Press, Reno, Las Vegas, London

Bernstein, E 1975 *Evolutionary Socialism: A Criticism and Affirmation*, Schoken Books, New York

Bernstein, J 1994 *Frankfurt School: Critical Assessments*, Routledge, London

Bidet, J Kouvelakis S 2008 'Introduction: Marxism, Post-Marxism, Neo-Marxisms' in J Bidet and S Kouvelakis (eds) *Critical Companion to Contemporary Marxism*, Brill, Leiden and Boston: 23-38

Blackledge, P 2006 'The New Left's Renewal of Marxism' *International Socialism: A Quarterly Review of Socialist Theory*, Issue, 112, Retrieved 20 May 2019 http://isj.org.uk/issue-112/

Bloch, E 2015 'The Principle of Hope', *Marxists Internet Library*, Retrieved 22 November 2018 https://www.marxists.org/archive/bloch/hope/introduction.htm

Bonefeld, W 2006 'Anti-globalisation and the Question of

Socialism' Critique, vol. 31, no. 1: 39-59

Boucher, G 2012 *Understanding Marxism*, Acumen Publishing Ltd., Durham, UK

Bronner, SE 2011 *Critical Theory: A Very Short Introduction*, Oxford University Press, New York

Burawoy, M 1990 'Marxism is Dead, Long Live Marxism' *Socialist Review*, vol. 90 no. 2: 7-19

Burawoy, M Wright, EO 2006 'Sociological Marxism' in JH Turner (ed) *Handbook of Sociological Theory*, Springer, New York: 459-486

Calhoun, CJ 1997 *Nationalism*, University of Minnesota Press

Callinicos, A 1983 *Marxism and Philosophy*, Oxford University Press, Oxford and New York

Callinicos, A 1990 *Against Postmodernism: A Marxist Critique*, St Martin's Press, New York

Cammack, P 2003 'The Governance of Global Capitalism: A New Materialist Perspective' *Historical Materialism*, Vol. 11, no. 2: 37-59

Carr, EH, 1953 'Stalin', *Soviet Studies*, vol. 5, no., 1: 1-7

Carr, EH 1978 *Socialism in One Country, 1924-26: Volume I*, The Macmillan Press, London and Basingstoke

Castells, M 2004 *The Power of Identity: The Information Age: Economy, Society and Culture Volume 2*, 2nd edn Wiley & Blackwell, Malden MA, Oxford, Chichester, UK

Chodos, H 2007 'Marxism and Socialism' in D Glaser and DM Walker, *Twentieth-Century Marxism: A Global Introduction*, Routledge, Taylor and Francis, London and New York: 177-195

Chossudovsky, M 1998 *The Globalisation of Poverty: Impacts of IMF and World Bank Reforms*, Zed Books, London and New York

Collado, E 2010 *The Shrinking Middle Class: Why America is Becoming a Two-Class Society*, Universe, Bloomington, New York

Colletti, L 1974 'Bernstein and the Marxism of the Second

International' in L Colletti's collected essays *From Rouseau to Lenin: Studies in Ideology and Society*, Monthly Review Press, New York: 45-108

Communist Party of Australia 2016 *Policies, Communist Party of Australia, Retrieved* 6 August 2018 http://www.cpa.org.au/policies/index.html

Cox, RW 1987 *Production, Power and World Order: Social Forces in the Making of History*, Columbia University Press, New York

Credit Suisse 2015 *Global Wealth Report 2015*, Credit Suisse Research Institute, Retrieved June 23 2019 http://www.protothema.gr/files/1/2015/10/14/ekthsi_0.pdf

Crenshaw, K 1993 *Mapping the Margins: Intersectionality, Identity Politics, and Violence Against Women of Color*, Retrieved 15 November 2018, http://socialdifference.columbia.edu/files/socialdiff/projects/Article__Mapping_the_Margins_by_Kimblere_Crenshaw.pdf

Critchley, P 1997 *Beyond Modernity and Postmodernity: Vol. 1: Marx on the Postmodern Terrain*, Academia, Retrieved 22 May 2019 http://mmu. Academia.edu/PeterCritchley/Books

Dabla, E Kochhar, K Suphaphiphat, N Ricka, F Tsounta, E 2015 'Causes and Consequences of Income Inequality: A Global Perspective' *IMF Strategy, Policy and Review Department*, Retrieved 20 June 2019 https://www.imf.org/external/pubs/ft/sdn/2015/sdn1513.pdf

D'Amato, P 2006 *The Meaning of Marxism*, Haymarket Books, Chicago

Day, RB Gaido, D 2009 *Witnesses to Permanent Revolution: The Documentary Record*, Brill, London

Deutscher, I 1973 edited by T Deutscher *Marxism in Our Time*, Ramparts Press, San Francisco

Dunn, B 2009, *Global Political Economy: A Marxist Critique*, Pluto Press, London UK

Eagleton, T 1991 *Ideology: An Introduction*, Verso, London and New York

Engels, F 1966 *Socialism: Utopian and Scientific*, Progress Publishers, Moscow

Engels, F 1976 *The Dialectics of Nature*, Progress Publishers, Moscow

Engels, F 1984 *The Condition of the Working Class in England*, Progress Publishers, Moscow and Lawrence & Wishart, London

Engels, F 1986 'The Origin of the Family, Private Property and the State', in *Marx & Engels Selected Works*, Progress Publishers, Moscow: 449-583

Engels, F 2000 'A Letter to Franz Mehring' Retrieved 5 January 2019, *Marx-Engels Correspondence 1893*, http://www.marxists.org/archive/marx/works/1893/letters/93_07_14.htm

Engels, F 2010 'The Principles of Communism' in *Marx & Engels Collected Works Vol. 6*, Lawrence & Wishart, UK: 341-357

European Commission (2016). Innovation Policy. http://ec.europa.eu/enterprise/policies/innovation/policy/innovationnion/index_en.htm accessed 2 June 2019

Farred, G 2000 'Endgame Identity? Mapping the New Left Roots of Identity Politics' *New Literary History*, vol. 31, no. 4: 627-648

Femia, J 2007 'Western Marxism' in D Glaser and DM Walker (eds) *Twentieth-Century Marxism: A Global Introduction*, Routledge Taylor and Francis Group London and New York: 95-117

Flacks, R 2004 'Knowledge for What? Thoughts on the State of Social Movement Studies' in J Goodwin and J Jasper (Eds), *Rethinking Social Movements: Structure, Meaning, and Emotion*, Lanham, MD: Rowman & Littlefield, Lanham, MD: 135-154

Fuentes-Ramirez, RR 2014 'Marxist Perspectives on Twenty-first Century Transition to Socialism' *Socialism and Democracy*, vol. 28 no. 1:123-142

Gamble, A 1999 'Why Bother with Marxism?' in A Gamble, D Marsh and T Tant (eds) *Marxism and Social Science*, University of Illinois Press, Urbana and Chicago: 1-8

Gamble, A 2009 *The Spectre at the Feast: Capitalist Crisis and the Politics of Recession*, Palgrave and Macmillan, Houndmills, Basingstoke, Hants, UK

Gills, BK and Gray, K 2012 'People Power in the Era of Global Crisis: Rebellion, Resistance, and Liberation' *Third World Quarterly*, vol. 33, no. 2: 205-224

Glynn, A Hughes, A Lipietz, Singh, A 1990 'The Rise and Fall of the Golden Age' in SA Marglin and JB Schor (eds) *The Golden Age of Capitalism: Reinterpreting the Postwar Experience*, Clarendon Press Oxford

Goodwin, J Jasper, JM 2009 'Editors' Introduction' in J Goodwin and JM Jasper (eds) *The Social Movement Reader: Cases and Concepts* 2nd edn., Wiley and Blackwell: 3-8

Gorz, A 1997 *Farewell to the Working Class*, Pluto Press, London

Gouldner, AW 1980 *The Two Marxisms: Contradictions and Anomolies in the Development of Theory*, Seabury Press, New York

Gramsci, A 1971 *Selections from Prison Notebooks*, Lawrence and Wishart, London

Guigni, M 1999 'Introduction: How Social Movements Matter: Past Research, Present Problems, Future Developments' in M Guigni, D McAdam, C Tilly (eds) *How Social Movements Matter*, University of Minnesota Press: xii-xxxiii

Hardt, M and Negri, A 2000 *Empire*, Harvard University Press, Cambridge Ma, London England

Harman, C 1999 *A People's History of the World*, Bookmarks, London, Chicago and Sydney

Harvey, D 2010 'Organizing For the Anti-capitalist Transition' *Interface: A Journal For and About Social Movements*, vol. 2, no. 1: 243-261

Harvey, D 2012 *Rebel Cities: From the Right to the City to the Urban Revolution*, Verso, London and New York

Hay, P 2002 *Main Currents in Western Environmental Thought*, UNSW Press Sydney

Hirst, P Thompson, G 1999 *Globalization in Question: The International Economy and the Possibilities of Governance*, 2nd edn., Polity Press, Cambridge, UK

Hobsbawm, E 2004 'Introduction: Inventing Traditions' in E Hobsbawm and T Ranger (eds) *The Invention of Tradition*, Cambridge University Press, Cambridge: 1-14

Holmes, P 2009 'Protectionism: Who Does it Really Protect?' *NATO Review*, Retrieved 23 July 2018, http://www.nato.int/docu/review/2009/FinancialCrisis/PROTECTIONISM/EN/index.htm

Horkheimer, M 1982 *Critical Theory: Selected Essays*, Continuum Publishers, New York

Howe, I Coser, L 1962 *The American Communist Party: A Critical History*, Frederick Praeger, New York

Hunt, SA Benford, RD 2007 'Collective Identity, Solidarity, and Commitment' in DA Snow, A Soule, H Kriesi (eds) *The Blackwell Companion to Social Movements*, Blackwell Publishers Ltd.: 433-457

Husson, M 2008 'The Regulation School: A One-Way Ticket from Marx to Social Liberalism?', in J Bidet and J Kouvelakis (eds) *Critical Companion to Contemporary Marxism*, Brill, Leiden and Boston: 175-188

Hyman, R 1975 *Marxism and the Sociology of Trade Unionism*, Pluto Press Ltd., London

Ignatow, G 2007 *Transnational Identity Politics and the Environment*, Lexington Books, a division of Rowman & Littlefield Inc., Lanham, Boulder, New York, Toronto, Plymouth UK

International Labour Office, 2008, *Global Wage Report*, Retrieved 13 February 2019 http://www.ilo.org/wcmsp5

International Labour Office, 2015 *World Employment and Social Outlook – Trends 2015*, Retrieved 21 May 2019 www.ilo.org/global/research/global-reports/WESO/2015/lang--en/index.htm

International Labour Organization/Organisation for Economic

Co-operation and Development 2015 'The Labour Share in G20 Economies' *ILO/OECD* Retrieved 20 July 2018 https://www.oecd.org/g20/topics/employment-and-social-policy/The-Labour-Share-in-G20-Economies.pdf

International Monetary Fund, 2016 'Subdued Demand, Diminished Prospects' *World Economic Outlook: Update January 2016*, Retrieved 3 March 2019, http://www.imf.org/external/pubs/ft/weo/2016/update/01/index.htm

Jay, M 1996 *The Dialectical Imagination: A History of the Frankfurt School and the Institute of Social Research*, 1923-1950 Heineman, London

Jellissen, SM and Gottheil, F 2009 'Marx and Engels: In Praise of Globalization' *Contributions to Political Economy*, vol. 28: 35-46

Jenkins, K 2005 *On 'What is History?': From Carr and Elton to Rorty and White*, Routledge, New York and London

Jotia, L 2011, 'Globalization and the Nation-State: Sovereignty and State Welfare in Jeopardy', *US-China Education Review B* 2: 243-250

Kelley, RDG 1997 'Identity Politics and Class Struggle' *New Politics*, vol, 6 no. 2 (Winter)

Kolakowski, L 1978 *Main Currents of Marxism: Its Rise, Growth, and Dissolution, Vol. 1*, Clarendon Press, Oxford

Kolakowski, L 2017 'Marxist Roots of Stalinism' in RC Tucker (ed) *Stalinism: Essays in Historical Interpretation*, Routledge, London and New York: 283-298

Koo, JH 2000 'The Dilemmas of Empowered Labor in Korea: Korean Workers in the Face of Global Capitalism' *Asian Survey*, vol. 40, no. 2: 227-250

Korsch, K 1931 'The Crisis of Marxism', *Marxists.org*, retrieved 6 November 2018, https://www.marxists.org/archive/korsch/1931/crisis-marxism.htm

Korsch, K 1950 'Ten Theses on Marxism Today' *Marxist Internet Archive*, Retrieved 7 May 2019, https://www.marxists.org/archive/korsch/1950/ten-theses.htm

Kotkin, S 2014 *Stalin: Paradoxes of Power, 1878-1928*, Penguin, New York

Laclau, E and Mouffe, C 2001 *Hegemony and Socialist Strategy: Towards a Radical Democratic Politics*, (2nd edn) Verso, London and New York

Laffey, M Dean, K 2002 'A Flexible Marxism for Flexible Times: Globalization and Historical Materialism' in M Rupert and H Smith (eds) *Historical Materialism and Globalization*, Routledge, Taylor & Francis Group, London and New York: 90-109

Lebowitz, MA 2004 'What Keeps Capitalism Going' *Monthly Review*, vol. 56, no. 2: 19-25

Lebowitz, MA 2012a 'What Makes the Working Class a Revolutionary Subject?' *Monthly Review: An Independent Socialist Magazine*, Vol. 64 No. 7: 35-37

Lebowitz, MA 2012b 'Change the System, Not its Barriers' in M Musto (ed) *Marx for Today*, Routledge, Taylor and Francis Group, London and New York: 59-72

Leisink, P 1999 'Introduction', in P Leisink (ed) *Globalization and Labour Relations*, Edward Elgar, Cheltenham, UK Northampton MA US: 1-35

Lenin, V 1932 *Letters from Afar*, International Publishers, New York

Lenin, V 1972 'For Bread and Peace' *Collected Works* vol. 26, Progress Publishers, Moscow

Lenin, VI 1977a 'The Three Sources and Three Component Parts of Marxism' in *VI Lenin Selected Works in Three Volumes, Volume 1*, Progress Publishers, Moscow

Lenin, VI 1977b 'Marxism and Revisionism' in *VI Lenin Selected Works in Three Volumes, Volume 1*, Progress Publishers, Moscow

Lenin VI 1977c 'The State and Revolution: The Marxist Theory of the State and the Tasks of the Proletariat in the Revolution', in *VI Lenin Selected Works in Three Volumes, Volume 2*, Progress Publishers, Moscow

Lenin, VI 1977d 'What Is To Be Done? Burning Questions of Our Movement' Outline in *VI Lenin Selected Works in Three Volumes, Volume 1*, Progress Publishers, Moscow

Little, D 1986 *The Scientific Marx*, University of Minnesota Press, Minneapolis

Lowenthal, R 1964 *World Communism*, Oxford University Press

Lozovsky, A [pseud. for Dridzo], SA 1976 *Marx and the Trade Unions*, Greenwood Press Publishers, Westport, Connecticut

Lubasz, H 1984 '*The Dialectical Imagination* by Martin Jay' in J Marcus and Z Tar (eds) *Foundations of the Frankfurt School of Social Research*, Transaction Books, New Brunswick USA: 79-92

Lukacs, G 1976 *History and Class Consciousness: Studies in Marxist Dialectics*, MIT Press, Cambridge Mass.

Lukacs, G 2000 *A Defence of History and Class Consciousness: Tailism and the Dialectic*, Verso, London and New York

Luxemburg, R 1982 *Reform or Revolution*, Pathfinder Press, New York

Lyotard, J-F 1984 *The Postmodern Condition: A Report on Knowledge*, University of Minnesota Press, Minneapolis

Macionis, JJ 2007 *Sociology* 11th edn., Pearson/Prentice Hall, New Jersey

Mann, M 1973 *Consciousness and Action among the Western Working Class*, Macmillan, London

Marcuse, H 1972 *One Dimensional Man*, Abacus, London

Markovic, M 2017 'Stalinism and Marxism' in RC Tucker (ed) *Stalinism: Essays in Historical Interpretation*, Routledge, London and New York: 299-319

Martin, HP and Schumann, H 1997 *The Global Trap*, Zed Books, London and New York

Marx, K 1918 *A Contribution to the Critique of Political Economy*, Charles H Kerr and Company, Chicago

Marx, K 1956 *The Poverty of Philosophy*, Lawrence and Wishart, London

Marx, K 1968 *Theories of Surplus Value*, Volume 2, Progress Publishers, Moscow

Marx, K 1969a *Economic and Philosophic Manuscripts of 1844*, International Publishers, New York

Marx, K 1969b *Karl Marx On Colonialism and Modernization: His Despatches and Other Writings on China, India, Mexico, the Middle East and North Africa*, (ed with an introduction by S Avineri), Doubleday Anchor, New York

Marx, K 1974 *Grundrisse: Foundations of the Critique of Political Economy (Rough Draft)* Penguin Books, Harmondsworth, Middlesex, England

Marx, K 1986a *Capital: A Critique of Political Economy, Volume 1*, Progress Publishers, Moscow

Marx, K 1986b *Capital: A Critique of Political Economy. Volume 3*, Progress Publishers, Moscow

Marx, K 1986d 'Wages, Prices and Profit' in *Marx Engels Selected Works*, Progress Publishers, Moscow: 185-226

Marx, K 1986e 'The Eighteenth Brumaire of Louis Bonaparte' *in Marx Engels Selected Works*, Progress Publishers, Moscow: 94-179

Marx, K 2006 'Address of the Central Committee to The Communist League', *Marxist Internet Archive*, 2006, accessed 2 June 2019 https://www.marxists.org/archive/marx/works/1847/communist-league/1850-ad1.htm

Marx, K and Engels, F 1964 *The German Ideology*, Progress Publishers Moscow

Marx, K and Engels, F 1975 *Articles on Britain*, Progress Publishers, Moscow

Marx, K and Engels, F 1977 *Manifesto of the Communist Party*, Progress Publishers, Moscow

McCarney, J 1990 *Social Theory and the Crisis in Marxism*, Verso, London and New York

McIlroy, J Campbell, A 2019 'Bolshevism, Stalinism and the Comintern: A Historical Controversy Revisited' *Labor History*, vol. 60, no. 3: 165-192

Moore, B Jr 1978 *Injustice: The Social Bases of Obedience & Revolt*, The Macmillan Press Ltd., London

Moran, M 2015 *Identity and Capitalism*, Sage Publishers, Los Angeles, New Delhi, Singapore, Washington DC

Munck, R 2010 'Marxism and Nationalism in the Era of Globalization' *Monthly Review: An Independent Socialist Magazine*, Vol. 52 No. 3: 45-53

Naes, A 1973 'The Shallow and the Deep, Long-range Ecology Movement. A summary' *Inquiry* vol. 16, no. 1-4: 95-100

Nash, K 2000, *Contemporary Political Sociology: Globalization, Politics, and Power*, Blackwell Publishers, Malden Mass and Oxford

Newport, F 2015 'Fewer Americans Identify as Middle Class in Recent Years' Gallup Retrieved 27 October 2018, http://www. gallup.com/poll/182918/fewer-americans-identify-middle-class-recent-years.aspx

North, D 2014 *The Russian Revolution and the Unfinished Twentieth Century*, Mehring Books, Oak Park MI

Olofsson, G 1988 'After the Working-Class Movement? What's "New" and What's "Social" in the New Social Movements' *Acta Sociologica*, vol. 31, no. 1: 15-34

Organisation For Economic Cooperation And Development, 2014 'Focus on Inequality and Growth' *OECD Directorate for Employment, Labour and Social Affairs*, Retrieved 20 May 2019 www.OECD. Org/Social/Focus-Inequality-and-Growth_2014. PDF

Oxfam 2016 *An Economy for the 1%: How Privilege and Power in the Economy Drive Extreme Inequality and How this Can Be Stopped*, 210 Oxfam Briefing Paper, January 2016 Retrieved July 7 2018 https://www.oxfam.org/sites/www.oxfam.org/files/file_attachments/bp210-economy-one-percent-tax-havens-180116-en_0.pdf

Pannekoek, A 1915 'Marxism as Action', *Marxist Internet Archive*,

Retrieved 25 September 2018, https://www.marxists.org/ archive/pannekoe/1915/marxism-action.htm

Parkin, F 1968 *Middle Class Radicalism: The Social Bases of the British Campaign for Nuclear Disarmament*, University of Manchester Press, Manchester, UK

Pateman, C 1988 *The Sexual Contract*, Polity Press, Cambridge UK

Pettifor, A 2008 'Economies of Scale' *The Guardian*, retrieved 9 August 2018, https://www.theguardian.com/ commentisfree/2008/oct/21/globalisation-brettonwoods

Pieterse, JN 2002, 'Global Inequality: Bringing Politics Back In', *Third World Quarterly*, vol. 23, no. 6: 1023-1046

Piven FF 1995 'Globalizing Capitalism and the Rise of Identity Politics' *Socialist Register*, vol. 31: 102-116

Piven, FF Cloward, RA 1977 *Poor People's Movements: Why They Succeed, How They Fail*, Vintage Books, New York

Plekhanov, G 1976 *Selected Philosophical Works, Volume 3*, Progress Publishers Moscow

Popper, KR 1985 *Popper Selections* (ed D Miller) Princeton University Press, Princeton, New Jersey

Pryke, S 2012 'Economic Nationalism: Theory, History and Prospects' *Global Policy*, vol. 3 no. 3: 281-291

Ramos, V Jr 1982 'The Concepts of Ideology, Hegemony, and Organic Intellectuals in Gramsci's Marxism', *Marxists.Org*, Retrieved 15 April 2019, https://www.marxists.org/history/ erol/periodicals/theoretical-review/1982301.htm

Rees, J 1998 *The Algebra of Revolution: The Dialectic and the Classical Marxist Tradition*, Routledge, London and New York

Renton, D 2002 *Classical Marxism: Socialist Theory and the Second International*, New Clarion Press, Cheltenham, UK

Renton, D 2005 *Marx on Globalisation*, Lawrence & Wishart, London

Robinson, WI 1998, 'Beyond Nation-State Paradigms: Globalization, Sociology, and the Challenge of Transnational

Studies', *Sociological Forum*, Vol. 13, No.4: 561-594

Robinson, WI 2004 *A Theory of Global Capitalism: Production, Class and State in a Transnational World*, Johns Hopkins University Press, Baltimore and London

Rocamora, J 2012 'People Power is Alive and Well' *Third World Quarterly*, vol. 33, no. 2: 201-204

Rockmore, T 2002 *Marx after Marxism: The Philosophy of Karl Marx*, Blackwell Publishers, Oxford, UK

Sayer, D 1985 'The Critique of Politics and Political Economy: Capitalism, Communism and the State in Marx's Writings of the mid-1840s' *The Sociological Review*, vol. 33, no. 2: 221-253

Shah, A 2011 'Corporate Power: Facts and Stats' *Global Issues* Retrieved 21 July 2018 http://www.globalissues.org/article/59/corporate-power-facts-and-stats#Concentrationoftransnationalcompanies

Silver, B 2006 *Forces of Labor: Workers' Movements and Globalization since 1870*, Cambridge University Press

Sim, S 2011 'Post or Past?: Does Post-Marxism Have any Future?' *Global Discourse: An Interdisciplinary Journal of Current Affairs and Applied Contemporary Thought*, vol. 2, no. 1: 12-23

Sitton, JF 2010 Marx Today: *Selected Works and Recent Debates*, Palgrave Macmillan, New York

Sklair, L 2000 'The Transnational Capitalist Class and the Discourse of Globalisation' *Cambridge Review of International Affairs*, vol.14, no.1: 67-85

Sklair, L 2002 *Globalization: Capitalism & Its Alternatives*, 3rd edn., Oxford University Press

Small, AW 1897 'The Meaning of the Social Movement' *American Journal of Sociology*, vol. 3, no. 3: 340-354

Smith, MEG 2014 *Marxist Phoenix: Studies in Historical Materialism and Marxist Socialism*, Canadian Scholars' Press Inc., Toronto

Socialist Alliance 2015 *Towards a Socialist Australia*, Socialist Alliance, Retrieved 6 August 2018 https://socialist-alliance.

org/documents/towards-socialist-australia

Socialist Alternative 2007 *Statement of Principles* Socialist Alternative, Retrieved 6 August 2018 http://www.sa.org.au/node/3924

Solomon, S Rupert, M 2002 'Historical Materialism, Ideology, and the Politics of Globalizing Capitalism' in M Rupert and H Smith (eds) *Historical Materialism and Globalization*, Routledge, London and New York: 284-300

Strange, S 1997a *The Retreat of the State: The Diffusion of Power in the World Economy*, Cambridge University Press

Strange, S 1997b 'The Erosion of the State' *Current History*, vol. 96, no. 613: 365-369

Summers, L 2015 'The Global Economy is in Serious Danger' *Washington Post* 7 October 2015, Retrieved 3 March 2019, https://www.washingtonpost.com/opinions/the-global-economy-is-in-serious-danger/2015/10/07/85e81666-6c5d-11e5-b31c-d80d62b53e28_story.html

Swyngedouw, E 2010 'The Communist Hypothesis and Revolutionary Capitalisms: Exploring the Idea of Communist Geographies for the Twenty-first Century' in N Castree, P Chatterton, N Hynen, W Warner and MW Wright (eds) *The Point Is To Change It: Geographies of Hope and Survival in an Age of Crisis*, Wiley Blackwell, Chichester UK: 298-319

Szakonyi, D 2007 'The Rise of Economic Nationalism under Globalization and the Case of Post-Communist Russia' *Vestnik: The Journal of Russian and Asian Studies*, 16 May 2007

Tabb, WK 2010 'Marxism, Crisis Theory and the Crisis of the Early 21st Century' *Science and Society* vol. 74, no. 3: 305-323

Tanzi, V 1998 'The Demise of the Nation-state?' *IMF Working Paper, WP/98/120*, International Monetary Fund, Retrieved 12 July 2018 https://www.imf.org/external/pubs/ft/wp/wp98120.pdf

Tarr, Z 2011 The Frankfurt School: *The Critical Theories of Max Horkheimer and Theodor W. Adorno*, Transaction Publishers,

New Brunswick, USA and London, UK

Taylor, JD (Dan) 2013 *Negative Capitalism: Cynicism in the Neoliberal Era*, Zero Books, Winchester, UK and Washington, USA

Therborn, G 2008 *From Marxism to Post-Marxism*, Verso, London

Therborn, G 2012 'Class in the 21st Century' *New Left Review*, vol. 78

Thompson, EP 1957 'Socialist Humanism: An Epistle to the Philistines', *Marxist Internet Archive*, Retrieved 20 May 2019 https://www.marxists.org/archive/thompson-ep/1957/sochum.htm

Trotsky, L 1953 *The First Five Years of the Communist International in Two Volumes: Volume II* Pioneer Publishers, New York

Trotsky, LD 1965 *The History of the Russian Revolution, Volume One*, translated from the Russian by Max Eastman, Sphere Books Limited, London

Trotsky, L 1970 *The Third International After Lenin*, Pathfinder Press, New York

Trotsky, L 1972 *On Marxism and the Trade Unions: Trade Unions in the Epoch of Imperialist Decay*, New Park Publications, London

Trotsky, L 1973 *The Bolsheviki and World Peace*, Hyperion Press Inc., Westport, Connecticut

Trotsky, L 1974 *Collected Writings and Speeches on Britain, in Three Volumes – Volume Two* edited by R Chappell and A Clinton, New Park Publication, London

Trotsky, L 1977 *The Transitional Programme for Socialist Revolution*, Pathfinder Press, New York

Trotsky, L 1996 'The War and the International' *Marxists' Internet Archive*, Retrieved 5 June 2019, http//ww.marxists.org/archive/Trotsky/1914/war

Trotsky, L 2006 'Presenting Karl Marx', in L Trotsky (ed) *The Essential Marx*, Dover Publications Inc., Mineola, New York: 1-43

Trotsky, L 2007 *The Permanent Revolution & Results and Prospects*, with an introduction by M Lowy, Resistance Books, London

Trotsky, L 2010 *The Permanent Revolution and Results and Prospects*, Red Letter Press, Seattle, US

van der Pijl K 2002 'Historical Materialism and the Emancipation of Labour' in M Rupert and H Smith (eds) *Historical Materialism and Globalization*, Routledge, London and New York: 129-146

van Ree, E 2010 '"Socialism in one country" before Stalin: German origins' *Journal of Political Ideologies*, vol.15, no. 2: 143-159

Wainwright, J Kim, SJ 2008 'Battles in Seattle *Redux*: Transnational Resistance to a Neoliberal Trade Agreement' *Antipode*, vol. 40, no. 4: 513-534

Walker, D 2015 'Towards a New Gospel of Wealth' Ford Foundation, Retrieved 2 November 2018, https://www. fordfoundation.org/ideas/equals-change-blog/posts/toward-a-new-gospel-of-wealth/

Wallerstein, I 1986 'Marxisms as Utopias' *American Journal of Sociology*, vol. 91, no. 6: 1296-1308

Warren, B 1980 *Imperialism: Pioneer of Capitalism*, NLB and Verso, London

Webster, E Lambert, R Bezuidenhout, A 2008 *Grounding Globalization: Labour in the Age of Insecurity*, Blackwell Publishing, Malden MA

Weisbord, A 1937 'The Conquest of Power' Marxists Internet Archive, Retrieved 17 March 2016, https://www.marxists.org/archive/weisbord/conquest17.htm

Wheelwright, EL 1953 'Trade Unions and the State' *The Australian Quarterly*, vol. 25, no. 2: 26-36

Wiggershaus R 1994 *The Frankfurt School: Its History, Theories and Political Significance,* Polity Press, Cambridge

Wolf, M 2004 *Why Globalization Works*, Yale University Press, New Haven Connecticut

Wood, EM 2002 'Global Capital, National States' in M Rupert and H Smith (eds) *Historical Materialism and Globalization,* Routledge, Taylor and Francis, London and New York: 17-39

Woods, A Grant, T 2007 *Lenin and Trotsky: What They Really Stood For*, Aakar Books, Delhi, India

WTO 2016 *Report on G20 Trade Measures (mid-October 2015 to mid-May 2016)* WTO-OMC, Retrieved 22 July 2018 https://www.wto.org/english/news_e/news16_e/g20_wto_report_june16_e.pdf

Yates, CAB 2003 'The Revival of Industrial Unions in Canada: The Extension and Adaptation of Industrial Union Practices to the New Economy' in P Fairbrother and CAB Yates (eds) *Trade Unions in Revival: A Comparative Study*, Routledge, Taylor and Francis Group, London and New York: 221-243

Author biography

William Briggs is a Marxist political economist with a special interest in political theory. He has a long history as a teacher and journalist in Australia and Moscow, where he lived and worked for 3 years. In more recent times he has been engaged as an academic, affiliated to Deakin University in Melbourne, Australia.

Also by William Briggs

Classical Marxism in an Age of Capitalist Crisis: The Past is Prologue, Routledge, 2019

Can capitalism survive?

Capitalism has always lived in and with crisis. Wars, revolutions, economic depression, the threat of nuclear annihilation and ecological disaster have all failed to break the dominance of this economic and political system.

This book returns to classical Marxism as a means of finding the way to challenge the rule of capitalism.

A search for 'something better', this volume is an engaging read for scholars, researchers and for all who share an interest in politics, political theory and socialism.

From the author

Thank you for purchasing Removing the Stalin Stain and thank you for engaging in what is an endless battle of ideas. If you have a few moments, please feel free to add your review of the book at your favourite online site for feedback. Also, if you would like to exchange views with me, don't hesitate to contact me at briggsw88@gmail.com

Sincerely

William Briggs

Culture, Society & Politics

The modern world is at an impasse. Disasters scroll across our smartphone screens and we're invited to like, follow or upvote, but critical thinking is harder and harder to find. Rather than connecting us in common struggle and debate, the internet has sped up and deepened a long-standing process of alienation and atomization. Zer0 Books wants to work against this trend. With critical theory as our jumping off point, we aim to publish books that make our readers uncomfortable. We want to move beyond received opinions.

Zer0 Books is on the left and wants to reinvent the left. We are sick of the injustice, the suffering, and the stupidity that defines both our political and cultural world, and we aim to find a new foundation for a new struggle.

If this book has helped you to clarify an idea, solve a problem or extend your knowledge, you may want to check out our online content as well. Look for Zer0 Books: Advancing Conversations in the iTunes directory and for our Zer0 Books YouTube channel.

Popular videos include:

Žižek and the Double Blackmain

The Intellectual Dark Web is a Bad Sign

Can there be an Anti-SJW Left?

Answering Jordan Peterson on Marxism

Follow us on Facebook
at https://www.facebook.com/ZeroBooks and Twitter at https://twitter.com/Zer0Books

Bestsellers from Zer0 Books include:

Give Them An Argument
Logic for the Left
Ben Burgis
Many serious leftists have learned to distrust talk of logic. This is
a serious mistake.
Paperback: 978-1-78904-210-8 ebook: 978-1-78904-211-5

Poor but Sexy
Culture Clashes in Europe East and West
Agata Pyzik
How the East stayed East and the West stayed West.
Paperback: 978-1-78099-394-2 ebook: 978-1-78099-395-9

An Anthropology of Nothing in Particular
Martin Demant Frederiksen
A journey into the social lives of meaninglessness.
Paperback: 978-1-78535-699-5 ebook: 978-1-78535-700-8

In the Dust of This Planet
Horror of Philosophy vol. 1
Eugene Thacker
In the first of a series of three books on the Horror of Philosophy,
In the Dust of This Planet offers the genre of horror as a way of
thinking about the unthinkable.
Paperback: 978-1-84694-676-9 ebook: 978-1-78099-010-1

The End of Oulipo?
An Attempt to Exhaust a Movement
Lauren Elkin, Veronica Esposito
Paperback: 978-1-78099-655-4 ebook: 978-1-78099-656-1

Capitalist Realism
Is There No Alternative?
Mark Fisher
An analysis of the ways in which capitalism has presented itself
as the only realistic political-economic system.
Paperback: 978-1-84694-317-1 ebook: 978-1-78099-734-6

Rebel Rebel
Chris O'Leary
David Bowie: every single song. Everything you want to know,
everything you didn't know.
Paperback: 978-1-78099-244-0 ebook: 978-1-78099-713-1

Kill All Normies
Angela Nagle
Online culture wars from 4chan and Tumblr to Trump.
Paperback: 978-1- 78535-543-1 ebook: 978-1-78535-544-8

Cartographies of the Absolute
Alberto Toscano, Jeff Kinkle
An aesthetics of the economy for the twenty-first century.
Paperback: 978-1-78099-275-4 ebook: 978-1-78279-973-3

Malign Velocities
Accelerationism and Capitalism
Benjamin Noys
Long listed for the Bread and Roses Prize 2015, *Malign Velocities*
argues against the need for speed, tracking acceleration
as the symptom of the ongoing crises of capitalism.
Paperback: 978-1-78279-300-7 ebook: 978-1-78279-299-4

Meat Market
Female Flesh under Capitalism
Laurie Penny
A feminist dissection of women's bodies as the fleshy fulcrum of
capitalist cannibalism, whereby women are both consumers and
consumed.
Paperback: 978-1-84694-521-2 ebook: 978-1-84694-782-7

Babbling Corpse
Vaporwave and the Commodification of Ghosts
Grafton Tanner
Paperback: 978-1-78279-759-3 ebook: 978-1-78279-760-9

New Work New Culture
Work we want and a culture that strengthens us
Frithjoff Bergmann
A serious alternative for mankind and the planet.
Paperback: 978-1-78904-064-7 ebook: 978-1-78904-065-4

Romeo and Juliet in Palestine
Teaching Under Occupation
Tom Sperlinger
Life in the West Bank, the nature of pedagogy and the role of a
university under occupation.
Paperback: 978-1-78279-637-4 ebook: 978-1-78279-636-7

Ghosts of My Life
Writings on Depression, Hauntology and Lost Futures
Mark Fisher
Paperback: 978-1-78099-226-6 ebook: 978-1-78279-624-4

Sweetening the Pill
or How We Got Hooked on Hormonal Birth Control
Holly Grigg-Spall
Has contraception liberated or oppressed women?
Sweetening the Pill breaks the silence on the dark side of hormonal
contraception.
Paperback: 978-1-78099-607-3 ebook: 978-1-78099-608-0

Why Are We The Good Guys?
Reclaiming your Mind from the Delusions of Propaganda
David Cromwell
A provocative challenge to the standard ideology that Western
power is a benevolent force in the world.
Paperback: 978-1-78099-365-2 ebook: 978-1-78099-366-9

The Writing on the Wall
On the Decomposition of Capitalism and its Critics
Anselm Jappe, Alastair Hemmens
A new approach to the meaning of social emancipation.
Paperback: 978-1-78535-581-3 ebook: 978-1-78535-582-0

Enjoying It
Candy Crush and Capitalism
Alfie Bown
A study of enjoyment and of the enjoyment of studying. Bown
asks what enjoyment says about us and what we say about
enjoyment, and why.
Paperback: 978-1-78535-155-6 ebook: 978-1-78535-156-3

Color, Facture, Art and Design
Iona Singh
This materialist definition of fine-art develops guidelines for
architecture, design, cultural-studies and ultimately social
change.
Paperback: 978-1-78099-629-5 ebook: 978-1-78099-630-1

Neglected or Misunderstood
The Radical Feminism of Shulamith Firestone
Victoria Margree
An interrogation of issues surrounding gender, biology,
sexuality, work and technology, and the ways in which our
imaginations continue to be in thrall to ideologies of maternity
and the nuclear family.
Paperback: 978-1-78535-539-4 ebook: 978-1-78535-540-0

How to Dismantle the NHS in 10 Easy Steps (Second Edition)
Youssef El-Gingihy
The story of how your NHS was sold off and why you will have
to buy private health insurance soon. A new expanded second
edition with chapters on junior doctors' strikes and government
blueprints for US-style healthcare.
Paperback: 978-1-78904-178-1 ebook: 978-1-78904-179-8

Digesting Recipes
The Art of Culinary Notation
Susannah Worth
A recipe is an instruction, the imperative tone of the expert, but this constraint can offer its own kind of potential. A recipe need not be a domestic trap but might instead offer escape – something to fantasise about or aspire to.
Paperback: 978-1-78279-860-6 ebook: 978-1-78279-859-0